Go Crochet!
SKILL BUILDER

30 Crochet-in-a-Day Projects to Take You From Beginner to Expert

ELLEN GORMLEY

CONTENTS

SKILL-BUILDING PROJECTS 16

Berry Parfait Sca

INTRODUCTION

Thirty days, thirty projects. What can you accomplish in a month?

In thirty days, beginners can exponentially improve their skills. In thirty days, seasoned crocheters can make a serious dent in their stash closets.

The goal of this challenge is to make thirty projects in thirty days. Of course you don't have to, but that's the challenge. Along the way, you'll stretch your skills or learn new ones. You'll have a wide variety of projects to give or to keep, and you'll gain a sense of accomplishment.

For beginners, this book is a great way to immerse yourself in many techniques and skills so that, on the other side of thirty days, you'll be a well-rounded and skilled stitcher.

For seasoned crocheters, this book is a fun way to test your mettle, to push beyond the ordinary and get excited to accomplish more!

Look at your calendar. Be judicious and place easier, smaller, quicker projects on days where you know you're already busy with other commitments. Schedule the longer or more complex projects or new-skill projects for days when you anticipate having more time. Look at your calendar for special days and birthdays. Can you match up any special days with the perfect project? Make efficient use of your time by working to your needs.

These projects are not only designed to be made in just one day; they are designed to be fun and provide a little instant gratification so you'll want to make them again and again. If you want to sell your finished items at bazaars and craft fairs, you'll have a table full of stock at the end of thirty days!

I know you're thinking, what does Ellen mean by "a day"? Is it twenty-four hours? Is it a work day? In general, when I say a project can be made in a day, it means that if I start a project at 10:00 A.M., then I work when I can, off and on, while cooking and going about my life and sleeping through the night, I should be able to finish stitching by 10:00 A.M. the next day. Longer or more difficult projects can be reserved for a day when I have a block of time to myself.

For instance, *The Pineapple Stolen Time Stole* may require a day when you have more time, but the *Cornelia Beaded Bracelet* can be crocheted the hour before a party when you want to bring a last-minute gift. Also, I admit, some people stitch faster than others. It's only a race if you make it one. Otherwise have fun.

Many of the projects in the book can be made *bigger*! But don't forget, bigger projects will take more time and more yarn. Take this into consideration when deciding to mega-size it.

While you are working on one project, flip through the others and see what you can do for another. Order yarn, gather supplies, watch tutorials online and make swatches in advance for future projects.

On each project page, take notes! What yarn did you use and did you like it? What would you do differently next time? Who did you make the project for and would you enjoy making it again? Throw a yarn label in the book for that page. Make the book work for you!

When you are done, if you complete the thirty projects in thirty days, write to me and I'll give you a Crochet Champion Shout-out on my blog!

Need fodder for your own crochet blog? Keep status bars on the projects and update your readers with your efforts. Challenge your crochet pals to a Crochet Challenge Throwdown!

Dedication

Thank you, again, God. I often wonder why, of all the skills in the world, crochet is my talent. It's silly to question it. If I'm inspired in a creative way, I'll go with it. Lead the way.

Thank you to my family, especially my husband, Tom. Your hard work providing for me and the kids has enabled me to create not just crochet projects but a crochet career.

Thank you to my crochet friends and allies (in no particular order): Rebecca, Haley, Doris, Tammy, Robyn, Marly, Candi, Carol and the staff at Silk Road Textiles.

MATERIALS & TOOLS

Choosing Fibers

I chose yarns for this book based on their suitability for the projects. I also worked to use a variety of yarns with a variety of weights and prices. As you work through the book and the projects, you get to choose which yarn and colors you want to use to make your project unique. Substituting yarn takes a little consideration.

When choosing a yarn to use other than the specified yarn, it's important to match the fiber and gauge to get the closest result to the photo. A team of consultants for the Craft Yarn Council of America created a scale that describes the range of yarn weights. Categories are defined based on the number of single crochet stitches that are made per 4" (10.2cm). Worsted weight yarn is a "4" and bulky is a "5." Super-bulky is a "6." See the Craft Yarn Council's website, yarnstandards.com, for the full chart.

Some yarns will have an icon of a skein of yarn with a number from 1–6 on the label. This is the symbol for the yarn weight that corresponds to the Craft Yarn Council's chart. If the yarn does not have the yarn skein graphic on it, you can make a swatch from your stash to see how many single crochets work up in a 4" (10.2cm) swatch and compare it to the Craft Yarn Council's chart. This way you will know what size yarn you have in your stash, even if the label is lost.

When substituting yarn, choose a new yarn that is the same weight category as the yarn specified in the pattern. Also, make sure the new yarn is the same or similar fiber content as the specified yarn. Then make a swatch. There are only six yarn weight categories, but each worsted yarn on your shelf will be a little different from the others.

What is a similar fiber? If the yarn in the pattern is an animal fiber like wool, then make sure you choose another animal fiber when substituting. Good choices would be wool, alpaca, mohair or angora. If the yarn in the pattern is a plant fiber like silk, then make sure you choose another plant fiber when substituting. Good choices might be silk, bamboo or cotton. Cotton and bamboo behave differently, however, and a swatch will help you decide if it's the right choice for your project.

Stick to the same texture when choosing a substitute yarn. If the project is a fuzzy mohair, then choose a substitute that will have a similar texture. If the project calls for a sleek, smooth yarn, then you may not be happy with the results if you make the project in a fuzzy or nubby yarn.

Hooks

Just like yarn, hooks come in a wide variety of materials and prices. Whichever hook you swatch and start your project with is the one you should stitch and finish your project with. If you can't remember, make a note or take a digital photo of your hook with the swatch and yarn band so that you have a visual reminder of many useful details.

Crochet hook sizes range from tiny steel hooks to much larger hooks. The larger the hook, the larger the stitch will be. A hook is measured in millimeters (mm).

The letter or number of the hook may vary depending on the brand and country in which it was made. The millimeter number is the most reliable method of identifying a hook.

Tunisian Hooks

A few of the projects in this book use a Tunisian or afghan hook. For narrow projects, you might be able to improvise and use a traditional short crochet hook that does not have a thumb grip (the hook must have the same diameter for the entire length). Wider projects will need a special hook. Generally, the pattern will specify the length of hook that is needed. As a rule of thumb, choose a hook that is the width of the widest piece you will be working or slightly shorter. You can squeeze a pretty good number of stitches on a hook because of the squishiness of the yarn. Tunisian hooks also come with interchangeable and flexible cables for very wide projects or projects that are worked in the round. Read the materials list for each project before you begin to make sure you have the proper tools.

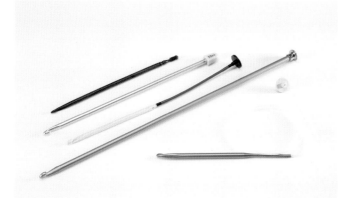

Yarn Needle

Whether you call it a yarn needle or a tapestry needle, this is an invaluable tool for weaving in ends. You'll want to have a few in case you drop one in the couch. Some stitchers use a latch hook tool, commonly used to make hooked rugs, to weave in ends. The latch hook tool has a much bigger handle and is less likely to be lost in the sofa. I use my bent tip yarn needles for weaving in ends more than any other tool. A measuring tape, ruler, scissors, and stitch markers are other items that are handy for all crochet projects.

Blocking Board and Rustproof Pins

Blocking is the process of setting the stitches in place either by wetting down or steaming the fabric and allowing it to dry to the desired measurements. Generally, most stitchers only "block" natural fibers and not acrylic, though many people believe blocking acrylic yarns adds to their softness. To block a crocheted piece, it needs a place to lie flat while it is wet and held in place with pins or wires. Fancy yarn stores sell interlocking foam mats that are ideal for blocking, but hardware and toy stores often sell cheaper and more colorful ones! Wet a project by spritzing it with water, soaking in water or steaming with a handheld steamer, then pin the dampened crochet piece to the mats with rustproof pins (because no one wants rust stains on the yarn). Blocking wires are long, thin wires that can hold larger crocheted pieces with straight edges. Flexible wires are also available.

BASIC CROCHET INSTRUCTIONS

SLIP KNOT

Every crochet project begins with a slip knot on the hook.

With the index finger extended, pinch the cut end of the yarn between the thumb and middle finger and loop up over the index finger. Wind the cut end around the thumb, and thread it under

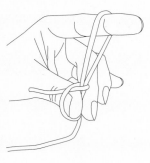

the index finger and behind the yarn loop. Put the cut end through the loop made by the thumb, withdraw the thumb and pull the cut end secure. Place the hook through the loop held by the index finger. Gently pull on the working end of the yarn to tighten the loop around the hook.

YARN OVER (YO)

Wrap the yarn around the hook and grab the yarn with the hook. To yarn over more than one time, wrap the yarn around the hook the indicated number of times.

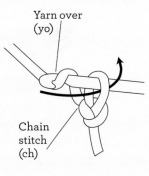

Yarn over (yo)

Chain stitch (ch)

CHAIN (CH)

With a slip knot on the hook, *grab the working end of the yarn with the hook and pull it through the loop on the hook. One chain made. Repeat from * as many times as instructed.

SLIP STITCH (SL ST)

Most commonly, a slip stitch is used to join rounds or to advance the yarn to the next spot where it is more convenient.

Insert the hook into the indicated stitch or space, then grab the yarn with the hook and pull it through both the stitch and the loop on the hook in one motion.

SINGLE CROCHET (SC)

Insert the hook into the next stitch, yarn over and pull up a loop through the stitch, yarn over and pull through both loops on the hook.

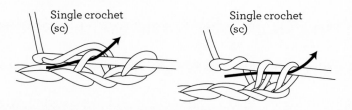

Single crochet (sc)

Single crochet (sc)

REVERSE SINGLE CROCHET OR CRAB STITCH (REV SC)

Right-handed: Stitches are normally worked counter-clockwise. To work in the reverse, go clockwise.
Left-handed: Stitches are normally worked clockwise. To work in the reverse, go counterclockwise.

Whichever hand you use, it's a little awkward to go the "wrong" way. Stitches are supposed to be somewhat lumpy and will look different. Follow the instructions for the single crochet but, instead of inserting the hook in the next space or stitch as usual, go backwards a space or stitch and put the hook there. This is a great finishing edging.

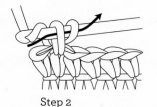

Step 1

Step 2

Step 3

HALF DOUBLE CROCHET (HDC)

Yarn over, insert the hook into the next stitch, yarn over and pull up a loop through the stitch, yarn over and pull through all three loops on the hook.

DOUBLE CROCHET (DC)

Yarn over, insert the hook into the next stitch, yarn over and pull up a loop through the stitch, yarn over and pull through two loops on the hook, yarn over and pull through the remaining two loops on the hook. On the post of the stitch, you can see one diagonal wrap of yarn indicating that you yarned over once when you began the stitch. Now you can tell by looking at the stitch that it is a double crochet.

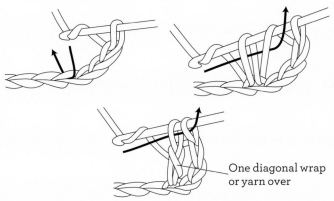

One diagonal wrap or yarn over

DOUBLE TREBLE CROCHET (DTR)

Yarn over three times, insert the hook into the next stitch, yarn over and pull up a loop through the stitch, yarn over and pull through two loops on the hook, yarn over and pull through two loops on the hook again, yarn over and pull through two loops on the hook a third time, yarn over and pull through two loops on the hook a fourth time. You can see on the tall post of the stitch three diagonal wraps of yarn indicating that you yarned over three times when you began the stitch. Now you can tell by looking at the stitch that it is a double treble crochet.

FRONT POST DOUBLE CROCHET (FPDC)

Yarn over, insert the hook from front to back around the post of the next stitch, yarn over and pull up a loop, (yarn over and pull through two loops on the hook) twice.

BACK POST DOUBLE CROCHET (BPDC)

Yarn over, insert the hook from back to front around the post of the next stitch, yarn over and pull up a loop, (yarn over and pull through two loops on the hook) twice.

TREBLE (OR TRIPLE) CROCHET (TR)

Yarn over twice, insert the hook into the next stitch, yarn over and pull up a loop through the stitch, yarn over and pull through two loops on the hook, yarn over and pull through two loops on the hook again, yarn over and pull through two loops on the hook a third time. You can see on the tall post of the stitch two diagonal wraps of yarn indicating that you yarned over twice when you began the stitch. Now you can tell by looking at the stitch that it is a treble crochet.

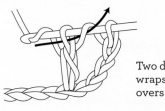
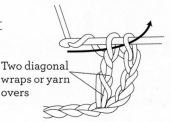

Two diagonal wraps or yarn overs

- -

POST STITCHES

- -

All post stitches are made like regular stitches except where you insert the hook at the beginning of the stitch. Usually, when you insert your hook to begin a stitch, the hook goes in the top two loops of the stitch beneath it. For any front post stitch, insert the hook from the front of the fabric that is currently facing you, around the post of the indicated stitch from right to left, yarn over and complete the stitch as usual.

For any stitch that is a back post stitch, insert the hook from the back of the fabric, around the post of the indicated stitch from right to left, yarn over and complete the stitch as usual. Post stitches can be decreased like regular stitches; the only difference is that the stitch is placed around the posts of the stitches below them instead of the top two loops of the stitch below.

CLUSTER (CL)

Yarn over, insert the hook in the stitch or space, yarn over and pull up a loop through the stitch, yarn over and pull through two loops on the hook (half of the stitch now made), yarn over, insert the hook in the same stitch or space, yarn over and pull up a loop through the stitch, yarn over and pull through two loops on the hook (half of the second stitch now made), yarn over, insert the hook in the same stitch or space, yarn over and pull up a loop through the stitch, yarn over and pull through two loops on the hook (half of the third stitch now made), yarn over and pull through all four loops on the hook. One cluster is complete.

BEGINNING CLUSTER (BEG-CL)

A beginning cluster is worked at the beginning of a round or row, and a ch-3 is used in place of the first double crochet to get you started.

Chain 3 (counts as the first double crochet), yo, insert the hook in the same stitch or space, yarn over and pull up a loop through the stitch, yarn over and pull through two loops on the hook (half of the second stitch now made), yarn over, insert the hook in the same stitch or space, yarn over and pull up a loop through the stitch, yarn over and pull through two loops on the hook (half of the third stitch now made), yarn over and pull through all three loops on the hook. One beginning cluster is complete.

 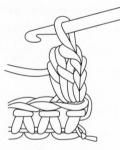

Beginning cluster
(beg-cl)

Beginning cluster
(beg-cl)

CLUSTERS

Clusters are multiple stitches decreased down to one that were all placed in the same stitch or space. Later, we'll talk about decreased or "together" stitches, which are the same as clusters except each stitch is in its own stitch or space. Typically clusters are made of multiple double crochet stitches, although clusters can also be made of treble and double treble crochet stitches. A cluster can be any number of stitches, though it is typically an odd number: three, five or (rarely) seven. If a pattern says cluster with no other explanation, it is assumed to be a cluster of three double crochets.

TREBLE CROCHET CLUSTER (3-TR CL)

*Yarn over twice, insert the hook in the st indicated, yarn over and pull up a loop, (yarn over and draw through two loops on the hook) twice; repeat from * two times more, yarn over and draw through all four loops on the hook.

Treble crochet cluster
(3-tr cl)

Treble crochet cluster
(3 tr cl)

BEGINNING TREBLE CROCHET CLUSTER (BEG 3-TR CL)

Chain four (counts as first treble crochet), *yarn over twice, insert the hook in the space indicated, yarn over and pull up a loop, (yarn over and draw through two loops on the hook) twice; repeat from * once more, yarn over and draw through all three loops on the hook.

INCREASE STITCHES

Increasing is easy! You've probably already been doing it by accident. When more than one completed stitch goes in the same place, it is increasing the number of stitches in the row or round. Corners are examples of stitch increases. In many of the motifs in this book, a corner is made by placing three stitches into the corner space, increasing by two more than on the previous round. Sometimes you will see increase written with the abbreviation inc.

SINGLE CROCHET DECREASE (SC2TOG)

(Insert the hook in the next stitch or space, yarn over and pull up a loop through the stitch) twice, yarn over and pull through all three loops on the hook.

DOUBLE CROCHET DECREASE (DC2TOG)

Yarn over, insert the hook in the next stitch or space, yarn over and pull up a loop through the stitch, yarn over and pull through two loops on the hook (half of the stitch now made), yarn over, insert hook in the next stitch or space, yarn over and pull up a loop through the stitch, yarn over and pull through two loops on the hook (half of the second stitch now made), yarn over and pull through all three loops on the hook. Two double crochets are now one stitch, and the stitch count is decreased by one stitch.

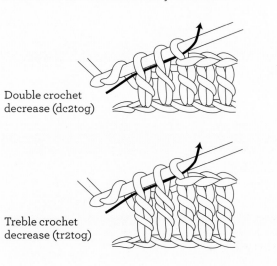

Double crochet decrease (dc2tog)

Treble crochet decrease (tr2tog)

DECREASE STITCHES

As explained in the cluster section, multiple stitches can be decreased or worked together into one. Sometimes you will see the abbreviation dc dec or dc2tog for two double crochets decreased into one. When you see dc dec, which is the traditional way of expressing a crochet decrease, decrease only one stitch. The instructions dc3tog and dc4tog are ways of decreasing three and four stitches, respectively, down to one. Similarly, other stitches can be decreased. Hdc2tog means to decrease two half double crochet stitches into one. Tr3tog means to decrease three treble crochet stitches into one. For the actual decreasing to happen, insert the hook to make the second half of the stitch in the next stitch or space, not in the same stitch or space like the cluster.

TREBLE CROCHET DECREASE (TR2TOG)

(Yarn over twice, insert the hook in the next stitch, yarn over, pull through the stitch, yarn over, pull through two loops on the hook, yarn over and pull through two loops on the hook again) two times, yarn over, pull through all three loops on the hook. Two treble crochet are now one stitch, and the stitch count is decreased by one stitch.

TRIPLE CROCHET DECREASE (TR3TOG)

Yarn over twice, insert the hook in the next stitch or space, yarn over and pull up a loop through the stitch, yarn over and pull through two loops on the hook, yarn over and pull through two loops on the hook again (half of the stitch now made), yarn over twice, insert the hook in the next stitch or space, yarn over and pull up a loop through the stitch, yarn over and pull through two loops on the hook, yarn over and pull through two loops on the hook again (half of the second stitch now made), yo twice, insert the hook in the next stitch or space, yarn over and pull up a loop through the stitch, yarn over and pull through two loops on the hook, yarn over and pull through two loops on the hook again (half of the third stitch now made), yarn over and pull through all four loops on the hook. Three treble crochets are now decreased to one stitch. The stitch count for the row or round has decreased by two stitches.

POPCORN STITCH (POP)

Generally, popcorn stitches are multiple completed stitches of the same type in the same stitch or space. If the pattern calls for a 5-dc pop, then make a double crochet in the next stitch, then another in the same stitch, then another, until you have five completed double crochet stitches in the same stitch. Here's the tricky part: gently remove the hook from the one remaining loop, insert the empty hook in the top two loops of the first double crochet of the five you just made, grab the dangling abandoned loop, yarn over and pull through the loop now on the hook. A finished popcorn stitch is usually followed by a chain or two. Allow the jumble of five double crochets to pop forward off the surface of the project.

POPCORN STITCHES

Most popcorn stitches are made with several complete stitches in one spot. After all the necessary stitches (usually three or five double crochets) are made in the same spot, they are tied together by removing the hook from the last stitch, inserting it in the top of the first stitch and also the top of the last stitch of the group, and pulling the working yarn through. This ties them into a neat package and makes them pop up from the surface of the fabric.

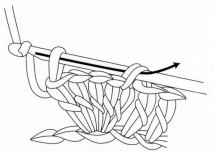

Popcorn stitch (pop)

BEGINNING POPCORN (BEG-POP)

Using the example above, the first of the five double crochets is replaced with a traditional chain three. This is used at the beginning of the row or round. Continue with the stitch by placing the remaining stitches in the same stitch or space and joining as described above. For a 5-dc beg-pop, you would chain three, work four double crochet in the same stitch, then proceed as with a regular popcorn.

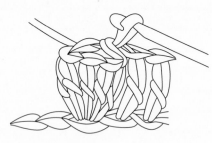

Popcorn stitch (pop)

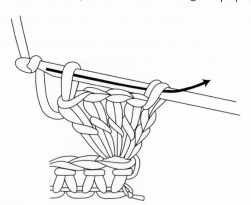

Begining popcorn (beg-pop)

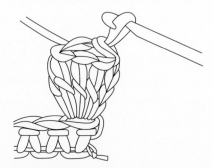

Begining popcorn (beg-pop)

Tunisian crochet has been called by other names, such as Shepherd's knitting or afghan crochet. Generally, a longer hook is used and loops are worked onto the hook across the fabric in a forward pass and then are bound off in a return pass. The work is not turned so that all the stitches are on the right or public side. The forward pass and return pass together make one complete row. The variety of stitches are made by where the hook is inserted in the fabric to pull up loops. Increasing and decreasing in Tunisian crochet can be done either on the forward pass or the return pass or both. All the traditional crochet stitches can also be used in Tunisian crochet to create variety and interest. It is very easy to count stitches in Tunisian crochet. When the forward pass is complete and all the loops of the row are held on the hook, each vertical loop on the hook is one stitch. Count loops at the end of each forward pass to maintain stitch count.

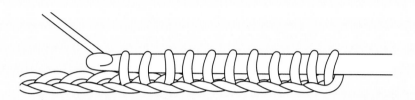

To begin Tunisian crochet, pull up a loop in each chain across. The number of loops will equal the number of chains.

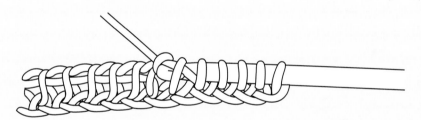

For the basic return pass, yarn over and pull through two loops on the hook.

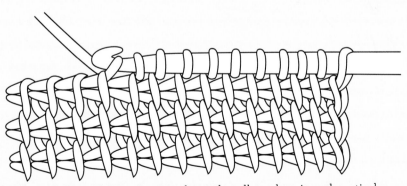

In the forward pass of Tunisian simple stitch, pull up a loop in each vertical bar across.

Stitch Diagrams

Most projects in this book have both written word instructions and diagrammed symbol instructions. The visual diagram is another way of communicating the same information as the written text. The stitch diagram offers another way to learn to make the project. You can refer to both sets of instructions or use only the one that is easier for you.

Each symbol in a stitch diagram represents one stitch. When following a stitch diagram in rounds, begin in the center and read the diagram outward in a counterclockwise direction. If you are left handed, you will read the diagram in a clockwise direction, the same as the way you work. Most of the projects are not turned; that is, all rounds are worked on the same, right, side. When the next round begins, the diagram will indicate the change with a change in color as well as the stitches needed to join and begin the new round. Row projects are turned.

Symbol diagrams for Tunisian crochet are only slightly different. Rows are generally not turned. Also, there is a wavy symbol over each stitch indicating the return pass.

Written Instructions

Each instruction begins with the yarn color, the hook size, and the number of beginning chain stitches. At the end of each row or round, a total count of each type of stitch and space is given. Count stitches and check work before continuing to the next instruction. Look at your work and compare it to the stitch diagram to see if it is correct. Parentheses are used to indicate that all the stitches within the parentheses should be put in the same stitch or space. For example, (sc, hdc, ch 2, hdc, sc) in the next ch-3 sp would mean to place all of those stitches, in that order, in the next ch-3 space. The difference between "ch-3" and "ch 3" is that the "ch-3" has already been made and "ch 3" is what you should do next. The dash makes all the difference.

Quick projects are often fun to make over and over again. Make a note of the yarns you used and any modification to hook size or methods in case you want to make the project again at a later date.

SAMPLE TUNISIAN STITCH DIAGRAM

Skill Levels

There is some discussion among crochet designers about skill levels. The Craft Yarn Council of America created the levels based on the competencies needed to complete the project. Some designers have their own way of categorizing project difficulty. Others would rather describe how much focused concentration is needed to complete the project. Is it something that can be crocheted while watching the kids or does it need to be worked in complete quiet with no distractions?

Personally, I believe that anyone can complete any project given enough support and time. Crochet is not that physically difficult, but it may take some practice and instruction. It may take a little longer when you have to learn new stitches first, but I'm not asking you to do a 540 on a snowboard. If you make a mistake, you can just rip it out. It's only yarn. If a project seems too intimidating at first, get the support of friends by making the project a "crochet-a-long." Work through the project together with each of you making your own project. But if you really want to understand the Craft Yarn Council skill levels, here they are:

1. *Beginner Projects* for first-time crocheters using basic stitches. Minimal shaping.

2. *Easy Projects* using yarn with basic stitches, repetitive stitch patterns, simple color changes and simple shaping and finishing.

3. *Intermediate Projects* using a variety of techniques, such as basic lace patterns or color patterns, midlevel shaping and finishing.

4. *Experienced Projects* with intricate stitch patterns, techniques and dimension, such as nonrepeating patterns, multicolor techniques, fine threads, small hooks, detailed shaping and refined finishing.

Here's a link to the Craft Yarn Council page on the subject: www.craftyarncouncil.com/skill.html.

Gauge

Gauge is the number of stitches in 1" (2.5cm) and the number of rows in 1" (2.5cm). Most patterns will present this information in terms of how many stitches in 4" (10.2cm). It may read: 12 sts and 12 rows = 4" (10.2cm).

This means that, if you take a hard ruler against your project, you should be able to count 12 stitches in 4" (10.2cm) and 12 rows in 4" (10.2cm) anywhere you measure. If you use the hook and yarn specified in the project and you are getting fourteen stitches, that's too many. That means your stitches need to be a little bigger so only twelve can fit in a 4" (10.2cm) space. You should swatch or make a practice piece with a bigger hook to get twelve stitches in 4" (10.2cm). If you are getting eight stitches in 4" (10.2cm) instead of twelve, then your stitches are too big, and you should try a smaller hook. The size of the rows is also important and needs to be adjusted to make gauge.

For most of the projects in this book, gauge is not critical. It is important, however, because you don't want to run out of yarn. The bigger the stitches, the more yarn is used. If you are making stitches substantially bigger than the gauge specified, you are going to run out of yarn quicker than if your stitches are the right size. Drape can also be affected by gauge. If your stitches are too small and tight, the fabric is going to be dense, stiff and drape less. Most accessories are designed to be loose and casual, but a tote bag might work better in a tighter fabric.

For motifs and projects worked in the round, gauge can be measured by the numbers of stitches and rows in 1" (2.5cm), but more commonly, gauge will be measured in rounds.

The only way you will be able to make sure you have the right gauge is to work a swatch, then measure frequently as you stitch the project. Block your swatch before you start the project in the same manner you expect to block your finished project. This will help you see the potential of your piece and make the best guess at how the finished project is going to look.

ABBREVIATIONS LIST

Bch: Bead chain

beg 3-tr cl: Beginning cluster of three trebles

beg 4-tr cl: Beginning cluster of four trebles

beg-cl: Beginning cluster (chain three and two double crochet in one stitch)

beg-pop: Beginning popcorn

blp(s): Back loop(s) only

BPdc: Back post double crochet

bsc: Bead single crochet

ch: Chain

cl: Cluster (three double crochet in one stitch)

dc: Double crochet

dc2tog: Double crochet decrease two together

dtr: Double treble crochet

edc: Extended double crochet

ehdc: Extended half double crochet

esc: Extended single crochet

Fdc: Foundation double crochet

flp(s): Front loop(s) only

FPdc: Front post double crochet

FPtr: Front post treble crochet

Fwd: Forward pass (Tunisian)

hdc: Half double crochet

inc: Increase

lp: Loop

pm: Place marker

pop: Popcorn

rem: Remaining

rep: Repeat

Ret: Return pass (Tunisian)

RS: Right side

sc: Single crochet

sh: Shell

sc2tog: Single crochet decrease two together

sk: Skip

sl st: Slip stitch

Tks: Tunisian knit stitch

Tps: Tunisian purl stitch

tr: Treble crochet

4-tr cl: Cluster of four trebles

3-tr cl: Cluster of three trebles

Tki: Tunisian knit increase

Tks: Tunisian knit stitch

tr2tog: Treble crochet decrease two together

tr3tog: Treble crochet decrease three together

Tss: Tunisian simple stitch

V-st: V stitch

WS: Wrong side

X-st: X stitch (Tunisian)

SYMBOL DIAGRAM KEY

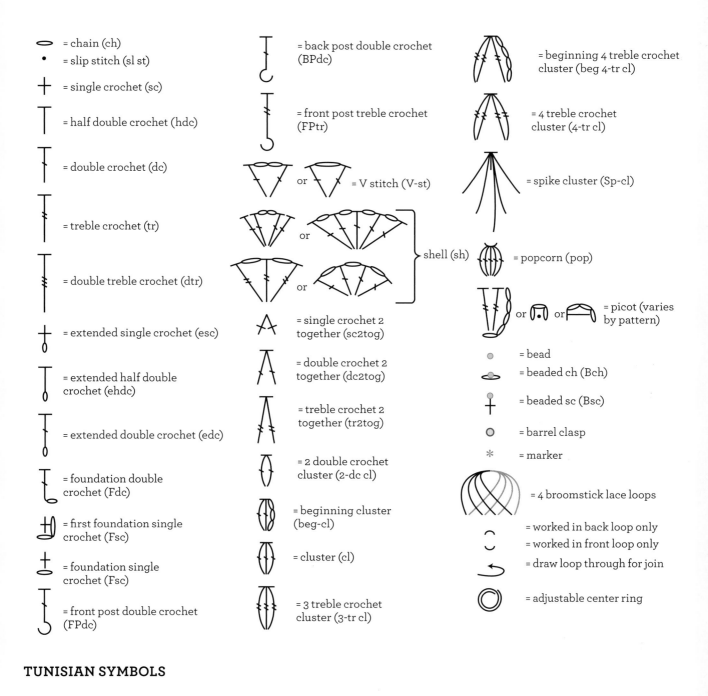

◯ = chain (ch)

• = slip stitch (sl st)

+ = single crochet (sc)

T = half double crochet (hdc)

T = double crochet (dc)

T = treble crochet (tr)

T = double treble crochet (dtr)

+ = extended single crochet (esc)

T = extended half double crochet (ehdc)

T = extended double crochet (edc)

T = foundation double crochet (Fdc)

= first foundation single crochet (Fsc)

+ = foundation single crochet (Fsc)

T = front post double crochet (FPdc)

= back post double crochet (BPdc)

= front post treble crochet (FPtr)

or = V stitch (V-st)

or / or = shell (sh)

A = single crochet 2 together (sc2tog)

A = double crochet 2 together (dc2tog)

A = treble crochet 2 together (tr2tog)

= 2 double crochet cluster (2-dc cl)

= beginning cluster (beg-cl)

= cluster (cl)

= 3 treble crochet cluster (3-tr cl)

= beginning 4 treble crochet cluster (beg 4-tr cl)

= 4 treble crochet cluster (4-tr cl)

= spike cluster (Sp-cl)

= popcorn (pop)

or or = picot (varies by pattern)

• = bead

◯ = beaded ch (Bch)

+ = beaded sc (Bsc)

◯ = barrel clasp

* = marker

= 4 broomstick lace loops

= worked in back loop only
= worked in front loop only

= draw loop through for join

◎ = adjustable center ring

TUNISIAN SYMBOLS

 = loop on hook at beg of round

= Tunisian knit stitch (Tks)

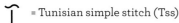 = Tunisian simple stitch (Tss)

= X stitch (X-st)

SKILL-BUILDING PROJECTS

There are a dozen different ways you could tackle the thirty projects in this book. You could start with the beginner items and move up to the more advanced ones, or you could dive head first into the projects with the stash and tools you have on hand. You can also look at your calendar and consider the birthdays and events you have coming up and tackle those gifts first. You could even work from the ground up, starting with the boot cuffs and working up to the hats. Items for the home could come next with the cup cozy and coasters. However you work through the projects, just start! With thirty different projects, you could choose at whim what strikes your fancy from day to day.

Pineapple Stolen Time Stole

I love that the pineapple is a symbol of welcome. I included it in this book because the pineapple is an essential part of crochet, but I had not stitched a pineapple project in years. Welcome back!

PATTERN NOTES
Beginning ch-3 counts as first double crochet.

Special Stitches
Shell (sh): ([dc, ch 1] 4 times, dc) in same st.

STOLE
Ch 38.

Row 1 (RS): Sc in 2nd ch from hook, [ch 3, sk 5 ch, sh in next ch, ch 3, sk 5 ch, sc in next ch] 3 times, turn.

Row 2: Ch 3, 2 dc in same st, *ch 1, [sc in next ch-1 sp, ch 3] 3 times, sc in next ch-1 sp, ch 1, [2 dc, ch 1, 2 dc] in next sc; rep from * to last sc, 3 dc in last sc, turn.

Row 3: Ch 3, 2 dc in same st, *ch 2, [sc in next ch-3 sp, ch 3] twice, sc in next ch-3 sp, ch 2, sk next ch-1 sp, [2 dc, ch 1, 2 dc] in next ch-1 sp; rep from * across to last dc, 3 dc in last dc, turn.

Row 4: Ch 3, 2 dc in same st, *ch 3 [sc in next ch-3 sp, ch 3] twice, [2 dc, ch 1, 2 dc] in next ch-1 sp; rep from * across to last dc, 3 dc in last dc.

Row 5: Ch 1, sc in 1st dc, *ch 3, sk next ch-3 sp, sh in next ch-3 sp, ch 3, sc in next ch-1 sp; rep from * across to last dc, sc in top of last dc, turn.

Rows 6–81: Rep Rows 2–5.

Rows 82–84: Rep Rows 2–4. Do not fasten off, continue to edging.

Edging
(WS) Ch 1, working down the long side, *work 2 sc in each row-end dc and 1 sc in each row-end sc across* to Row 1, ch 1.

Work across opposite side of foundation ch, sc in each ch across, ch 1.

Working up long side, rep from * to * across to last row, ch 1.

Working across the top of Row 84, sc 37 evenly across; join with sl st in 1st sc. Fasten off.

Finishing
Weave in ends.

FINISHED SIZE
› Before blocking: 8½" × 38½" (21.6cm × 97.8cm)

› After blocking: 10" × 45½" (25.4cm × 115.6cm)

MATERIALS
› Lorna's Laces Honor (3.5 oz/ 275 yds/251m/100g per ball): 1 hank #49 Periwinkle

› Size H/8 (5mm) crochet hook or size needed to obtain gauge

› Yarn needle

GAUGE
› 3 reps = 10" (25.4cm) after blocking

› 8 rows in pattern = 4" (10.2cm)

› Take time to check gauge

HOW TO MAKE A BASIC PINEAPPLE STITCH

1. While every pineapple pattern is different, they all start with basic crochet stitches.

2. Though it's a repeating pattern with multiple rows, take one row at a time.

3. In general, a pineapple pattern lengthens the space on the sides with chains and clusters the stitches toward the middle.

4. The final row of the repeat will set up the next repeat.

5. Compare your finished swatch with the stitch diagram.

PINEAPPLE STOLEN TIME STITCH DIAGRAM

EDGING

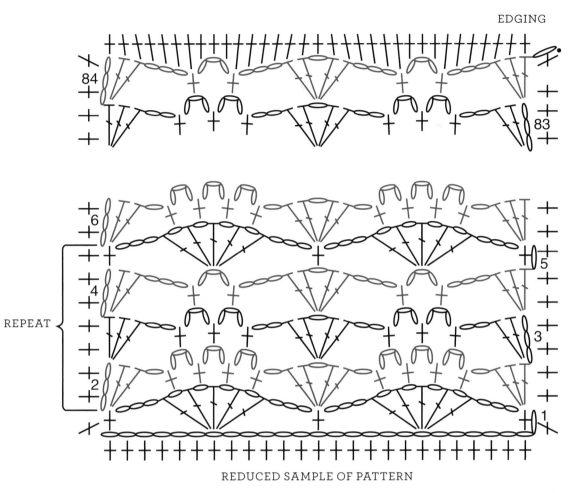

REDUCED SAMPLE OF PATTERN

Teardrop Earrings

Crocheted jewelry is popular right now, and it can be very dramatic. Jewelry findings are available at local craft stores, making it easy to coordinate a set of last minute earrings with an outfit.

PATTERN NOTES
All rounds are worked on the Right Side.

EARRINGS (MAKE 2)
With A, ch 5; join with sl st to form a ring.

Round 1 (RS): Ch 3 (counts as dc) 9 dc in ring; join with sl st in top 1st dc (10 dc). Fasten off A.

Round 2: With RS facing, join B with sc in any st, sc in each of next 3 sts, 2 dc in each of next 3 sts, sc in each of last 3 sts (13 sts). Sc in same st as 1st st of Round 2, ch 2; join with sl st in 1st sc. Fasten off.

Finishing
Weave in ends. Place kidney wire through ch-2 sp of each earring.

TEARDROP EARRINGS STITCH DIAGRAM

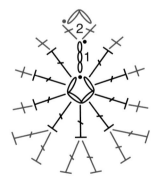

FINISHED SIZE
› 1¼" (3.2cm) at the widest point; 1½" (3.8cm) at the longest point

MATERIALS
› Universal Yarn, Nazli Gelin Garden 3, 100% Mercerized Egyptian Giza Cotton, (1.76 oz/136 yds/124m/50g per ball): 1 ball each #19 Light Tan (A) and #06 Deep Pink (B)

› Size E/4 (3.5mm) crochet hook or size needed to obtain gauge

› 2 kidney earring wires

› Yarn needle

GAUGE
› 2 rnds in pattern 1¼" (3.2cm) wide, 1½" (3.8cm) long

› Take time to check gauge

Apple Market Bag

Gala, Fuji, Granny Smith. . . . When I think of market bags, I think of apples! I can just imagine the Red Delicious apples shining through the easy mesh of this cotton bag. Just as the apple and the market bag are basic items, one of the basic skills you can learn in this project is the flat circle. Bookmark this page because you will use the first few instructions of the flat circle base over and over again in your crochet journey.

FINISHED SIZE

› 8½" × 12" (21.6cm × 30.5cm) (lying flat)

› Height is approximately 12¾" (32.4cm)

MATERIALS

› Blue Sky Alpacas Worsted Cotton (3.5 oz/150 yds/137m/100g per hank): 1 hank each of #603 Thistle (A) and #639 Wasabi (B)

› Size K/10½ (6.5mm) crochet hook or size needed to obtain gauge

› Yarn needle

› Locking stitch marker

GAUGE

› Base rnds 1–5 = 4" (10.2cm) in diameter

› Take time to check gauge

PATTERN NOTES

› All rounds are worked on the Right Side.

› Place marker in the first stitch of each round and move up as the work progresses.

Special Stitches

Foundation double crochet (Fdc): Yo, insert hook in base of last st made, yo, draw yarn through st, yo, draw yarn through 1 lp on hook (ch-1 made), [yo, draw yarn through 2 lps on hook] twice; *yo, insert hook in ch formed at base of last st made, yo, draw yarn through st, yo, draw yarn through 1 lp on hook (ch-1 made), [yo, draw yarn through 2 lps on hook] twice; rep for desired length.

BAG

With A, ch 5; join with sl st to form ring.

Round 1 (RS): Ch 1, 8 sc in ring; do not join (8 sc).

Round 2: 2 sc in each sc around (16 sc).

Round 3: [Sc in 1st st, 2 sc in next st] 8 times (24 sc).

Round 4: [Sc in next 2 sts, 2 sc in next st] 8 times (32 sc).

Round 5: [Sc in next 3 sts, 2 sc in next st] 8 times (40 sc).

Round 6: [Sc in next 4 sts, 2 hdc in next st] 8 times (40 sc, 16 hdc).

Round 7: [Sc in next 5 sts, 2 hdc in next st] 8 times (48 sc, 16 hdc).

Round 8: [Sc in next 6 sts, 2 hdc in next st] 8 times (56 sc, 16 hdc).

Round 9: Sc in each st around; switching to B in final st (72 sc).

Round 10: With B, sc in each st around, switching to A in final st (72 sc).

Round 11: With A, sc in each st around, switching to B in final st (72 sc).

Begin Side Pattern

Round 12: *Sc in 1st st, ch 3, sk next 3 sts; rep from * around; join with sl st in 1st sc (18 ch-3 sp).

Round 13: Sl st into ch-3 sp, ch 3 (counts as 1st dc) 3 dc in 1st ch-3 sp, *ch 1, 1 dc in next ch-3 sp, ch 1**, 4 dc in next ch-3 sp; rep from * around, ending last rep at **; join with sl st in top of beg ch-3.

Round 14: Ch 1, sc in 1st st, ch 3, sk next 3 dc *sc in next ch-1 sp, ch 3; rep from * around to last ch-1 sp, sk last ch-1 sp; join with sl st in 1st sc.

Round 15: Sl st into ch-3 sp, ch 4 (counts as 1st dc plus ch 1) *4 dc in next ch-3 sp, ch 1**, dc in next ch-3 sp, ch 1; rep from * around, ending last rep at **; join with sl st in 3rd ch of beginning ch-4.

Round 16: Ch 1, sc in 1st ch-1 sp, ch 3, *sc in next ch-1 sp, ch 3; rep from * around; join with sl st in 1st sc.

Rounds 17–28: Rep Rounds 15 and 16 (6 times).

Round 29: Rep Round 15.

Round 30: Ch 3 (counts as dc), dc in each ch and dc around, switching to A in last st; join with sl st in top of beg ch-3 (56 dc).

Round 31: With A, ch 1, sc in each st around, switching to B in last st; join with sl st in 1st sc (56 sc).

Round 32: With B, ch 3 (counts as dc), dc in next 4 sts, ch 2, sk next 2 sts, *dc in next 5 sts, ch 2, sk next 2 sts; rep from * around, switching to A in last st; join with sl st in top beg ch-3 (8 ch-2 drawstring sps).

Round 33: With A, ch 1, sc in each st and ch around; join with sl st in 1st sc.

Round 34: Ch 1, *(sc, ch 2, sc) in sc, sk next st, rep from * around; join with sl st in 1st sc. Fasten off.

DRAWSTRING STRAP

Row 1: With A, work 106 Fdc. Fasten off, leaving a sewing length. Weave tail end in and out of the ch-2 sps in Round 32. Without twisting drawstring, sew ends together to form a joined strap. Fasten off. Weave in ends.

HOW TO MAKE A FOUNDATION CHAIN

1. Chain four.

2. Double crochet in the fourth chain from the hook.

3. Yarn over, insert the hook into the two bottom loops of the previous stitch (as shown by the pointing hook).

4 Yarn over, pull through one loop on the hook (base chain made), [Yo and pull through two loops] twice.

5. Repeat the process to create the number of stitches needed.

CLOSE-UP OF THE APPLE MARKET BAG STITCH PATTERN

1. One round creates chain spaces.

2. Double crochet groups and lone double crochets will be placed in the chain spaces of the previous round.

MARKET BAG STITCH DIAGRAM 1

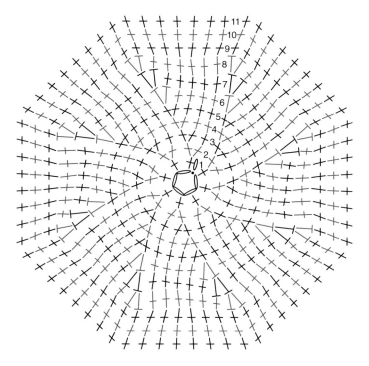

ROUNDS 1–11

MARKET BAG STITCH DIAGRAM 2

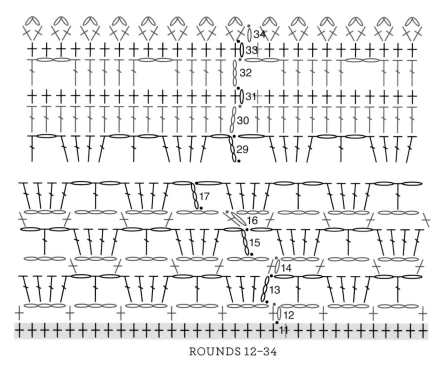

ROUNDS 12–34

Cottage Coasters

Felting is a skill you can practice with these adorable snapshots of crochet goodness. You can play with color or practice new stitches. Motifs are just tiny swatches. I think of them as yarn doodling. These coasters are small enough that it will be quick to whip up two of each and felt half to see what you learn!

FINISHED SIZE:
› **Coaster One before felting:** 5" (12.7cm) in diameter; after felting: 4" (10.2cm) in diameter

› **Coaster Two before felting:** 5" (12.7cm) in diameter; after felting: 4" (10.2cm) in diameter

› **Coaster Three before felting:** 5¼" (13.3cm) in diameter; after felting: 4⅓" (11cm) in diameter

MATERIALS
› **Classic Elite Yarns, Color By Kristin (1.75 oz/ 93 yds/85m/50g per ball):** 1 ball each #3215 Spring Green (A), #3236 Mushroom (B) and #3257 Cornflower (C)

› **Size I/9 (5.5mm) crochet hook** or size needed to obtain gauge

› Yarn needle

GAUGE
› **Coaster One:** Rounds 1–5 = 5" (12.7cm) in diameter

› **Coaster Two:** Rounds 1–3 = 5" (12.7cm) in diameter

› **Coaster Three:** Rounds 1–6 = 5¼" (13.3cm) in diameter

› **Take time to check gauge**

PATTERN NOTES

› All rounds are worked on the Right Side.

› All rounds are joined.

Special Stitches

Picot: Ch 3, sl st in 3rd ch from hook.

Beginning Cluster (beg-cl): Ch 3, [yo, insert hook in sp, yo, draw up a lp, yo, draw through 2 lps on hook] twice, yo and pull through 3 lps on hook.

Cluster (cl): [Yo, insert hook in sp, yo, draw up a lp, yo, draw through 2 lps on hook] 3 times in same sp, yo and pull through 4 lps on hook.

COASTER ONE

With A, ch 5; join with sl st to form a ring.

Round 1: Beg-cl in ring, ch 3 [cl, ch 3] 4 times in ring; join with sl st in top of beg-cl (5 cl; 5 ch-3 sps).

Round 2: With B, join with dc in any cl, 4 dc in next ch-3 sp, [dc in cl, 4 dc in next ch-3 sp] 4 times; join with sl st in top of 1st dc (25 dc). Fasten off.

Round 3: With RS facing, join A with sl st in any st, sl st in each st around; join with sl st in 1st sl st. Fasten off.

Round 4: Working behind the sl st in Round 3, with RS facing, join C with dc in any st, dc in same st, 2 dc in each st around; join with sl st in 1st dc (50 dc). Fasten off.

Round 5: With B, join with sc in any st, ch 2, sc in same st, sk next st, *(sc, ch 2, sc) in next st, sk next st; rep from * around, join with sl st in 1st sc. Fasten off.

COASTER TWO

With C, ch 5; join with sl st in 1st ch to form a ring.

Round 1: Ch 3, (counts as tr), 15 tr in ring, join with sl st in top of beg ch-3. Fasten off.

Round 2: With RS facing, join B with sc in any st, *ch 5, sc in next sc; rep from * around; join with sl st in 1st sc (16 ch-5 sps).

Round 3: With RS facing, join A with dc in any ch-5 sp, (picot, dc) in same st, (dc, picot, dc) in each ch-5 sp around; join with sl st in 1st dc. Fasten off.

COASTER THREE

With B, ch 8, sl st in 1st ch to form a ring.

Round 1: Ch 1, 12 sc in ring; join with sl st in 1st sc. Fasten off.

Round 2: With RS facing, join C with sl st in any sc, ch 3, (counts as dc), dc in same st, ch 2, sk next st; *2 dc in next sc, ch 2, sk next st; rep from * around; join with sl st in top beg ch-3. Fasten off.

Round 3: With RS facing, join A with sc in 1st dc of any 2-dc pair, sc in next dc, *ch 2, (cl, ch 3, cl) in next ch-2 sp, ch 2, ** sc in next 2 dc; rep from * around ending last rep at **; join with sl st in 1st sc. Fasten off.

Round 4: With RS facing, join B with sc in any ch-3 sp, 2 more sc in same sp, ch 5, sk next 2 ch-2 sps; *3 sc in next ch-3 sp, ch 5, sk next 2 ch-2 sps; rep from * around; join with sl st in 1st sc.

Round 5: Ch 3 (counts as dc), dc in next 2 sc, 6 dc in next ch-5 sp, *dc in each of 3 sts, 6 dc in next ch-5 sp; rep from * around, join with sl st in top of beg ch-3. Fasten off.

Round 6: With RS facing, join A with sl st in any st, sl st in each st around; join with sl st in 1st sl st. Fasten off.

Finishing

Weave in ends.

FELTING INSTRUCTIONS

With mild detergent and color-safe heavy fabrics, such as denim, machine wash in hot water. Check frequently for the desired degree of felting. Allow to agitate longer for more shrinkage. Do not tumble dry. Shape and lay flat. Weight coasters down with a heavy plastic bowl if necessary. Allow to air dry.

COASTER 1 STITCH DIAGRAM

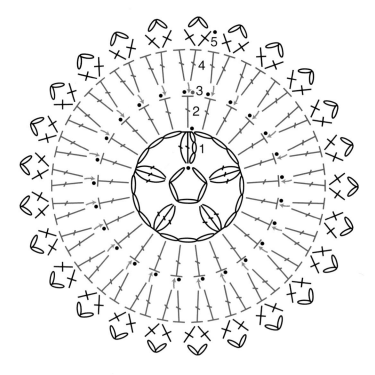

COASTER 1

COASTER 2 STITCH DIAGRAM

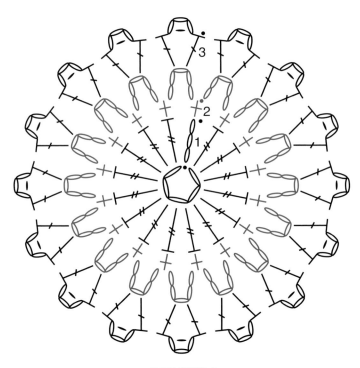

COASTER 2

COASTER 3 STITCH DIAGRAM

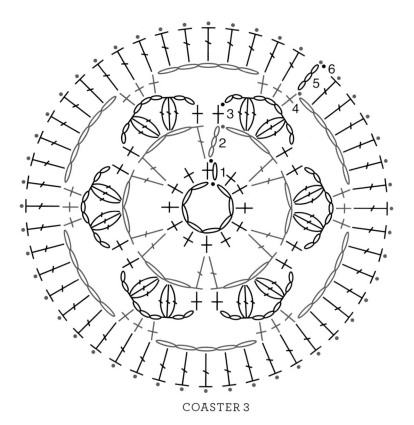

COASTER 3

SKILL LEVEL

Greased Lightning Hat

Extend your basic crochet knowledge with extended crochet stitches. Add some height and style with this vertically stitched hat. When working from the brim to the crown in turned rows through the back loop only, you'll learn how to create awesome stretch in crocheted fabric.

FINISHED SIZE:

› 20" (22") (50.8cm [55.9cm]) circumference

› Directions are given for size small. Changes for large are in parenthesis.

MATERIALS

› Red Heart Super Saver (7 oz/364 yds/ 333m/198g per skein): 1 skein each #3950 Charcoal (A) and #0316 Soft White (B)

› Size I/9 (5.5mm) crochet hook or size needed to obtain gauge

› Yarn needle

GAUGE

› 27 sts = 9" (22.9cm); 6 dc rows = 4" (10.2cm)

› Take time to check gauge

PATTERN NOTES
The hat is worked vertically in turned rows.

Special Stitches
Extended single crochet (esc): Insert hook in indicated st, draw yarn through st, yo, draw through 1 lp on hook, yo, draw through 2 lps on hook.

Extended half double crochet (ehdc): Yo, insert hook in next st, draw up a lp, yo, draw through 1 lp on hook, yo, draw through 3 lps on hook.

Extended double crochet (edc): Yo, insert hook in next st, draw up a lp, yo, draw through 1 lp on hook, [yo and pull through 2 lps on hook] twice.

HAT
With A, ch 28.

Row 1 (RS): Working in back ridge only of ch sts, sc in 2nd ch from hook and in each of next 6 ch, esc in each of next 4 ch, hdc in each of next 4 ch, ehdc in each of next 4 ch, dc in each of next 4 ch, edc in each of last 4 ch, turn (27 sts).

Row 2: Ch 3 (counts as edc), working in blps only, edc in each of next 3 sts, dc in each of next 4 sts, ehdc in each of next 4 sts, hdc in each of next 4 sts, esc in each of next 4 sts, sc in each of last 7 sts, turn.

Row 3: Ch 1, working in blps only, sc in each of 1st 7 sts, esc in each of next 4 sts, hdc in each of next 4 sts, ehdc in each of next 4 sts, dc in each of next 4 sts, edc in each of last 4 sts, turn.

Rows 4–5: With B, rep Rows 2 and 3.

Rows 6–29 (31): With A, rep Rows 2 and 3 (12 [13] times). Fasten off, leaving an 18" (45.7cm) tail. With yarn needle and tail, match sts from last row to Row 1 and whipstitch through both thicknesses.

Assembly
With yarn needle and A, weave yarn through every other st at top (sc) edge of hat. Gather rows tightly together and secure by weaving in ends.

Surface Crochet
With RS facing, join B at crown of hat on edge of B section. Work surface sl st down edge of the B stripe to brim. Rep for the other side of the B stripe. For help with the surface sl st, see photos of *Cabled Boot Cuffs*.

Edging
With RS facing, join A in side of any edc row on bottom edge of hat, ch 1, work 2 sc in each row-end st around; join with sl st in 1st sc (58 [62] sc). Fasten off.

Finishing
Weave in ends.

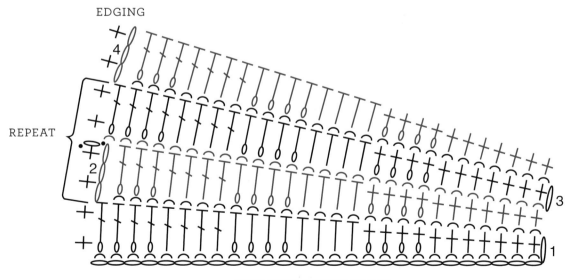

HAT STITCH DIAGRAM

HOW TO CREATE EXTENDED STITCHES

Extended Single Crochet (ESC)

1. Insert the hook in the indicated stitch, draw yarn through the stitch, yarn over, draw through one loop on the hook.

2. Yarn over, draw through two loops on the hook.

Extended Half Double Crochet (EHDC)

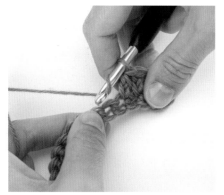  

1. Yarn over, insert the hook in the next stitch.

2. Draw up a loop.

3. Yarn over, draw through one loop on the hook.

4. Yarn over, draw through three loops on the hook.

Extended Double Crochet (EDC)

1. Yarn over.

2. Insert the hook in the next stitch, draw up a loop.

3. Yarn over and draw through one loop on the hook.

4. Yarn over.

5. Pull through two loops on the hook.

6. Yarn over, pull through two loops on the hook a second time to complete the stitch.

Berry Parfait Scarf

Crochet rows and crochet motifs can be friends! Learn how to coordinate both for whimsical results in this beginner scarf. Make it even easier by using just one color for an elegant accessory.

PATTERN NOTES

> › Scarf is worked in turned rows. The motifs are made separately and whipstitched onto the scarf.
> › An edging is added after assembly.
> › All motif rounds are worked on the Right Side without turning.
> › Join with a slip stitch unless otherwise stated.

Special Stitches

Beginning Cluster (beg-cl): Ch 3, [yo, insert hook in same sp, yo, draw up a lp, yo, draw through 2 lps on hook] twice, yo, draw through 3 lps on hook.

Cluster (cl): [Yo, insert hook in sp, yo, draw up a lp, yo, draw through 2 lps on hook] 3 times in same sp, yo, draw through 4 lps on hook.

SCARF

With A, ch 17.

Row 1 (RS): Working in back ridge of each ch, dc in 4th ch from hook and in each ch across, turn (15 dc). Fasten off.

Row 2: Ch 1, sc in flps only of each st across, changing to B in last st, turn. Fasten off A (15 dc).

Row 3: With B, ch 3, working in both lps of sts, dc in each st across, turn (15 dc).

Row 4: Ch 1, turn, sc in flps only of each st across, changing to C in last st, turn (15 sc).

Row 5: With C, ch 1, working in both lps of sts, sc across, turn.

Row 6: Ch 1, turn, sc in flps only of each sc across, changing to D in last st, turn.

Row 7: With D, ch 3, working in both lps of sts, dc in each st across, turn.

Row 8: With D, ch 1, sc in flps only of each st across, changing to A in last st, turn.

Row 9: With A, ch 3, working in both lps of sts, dc in each st across, turn.

Row 10: With A, ch 1, sc in flps only of each st across, changing to B in last st, turn.

Rows 11–82: Rep Rows 3–10 (9 times). Fasten off.

FINISHED SIZE

> › 5½" × 43" (14cm × 109.2cm)

MATERIALS

> › Plymouth Encore Worsted (3.5 oz/ 200 yds/183m/100g per ball): 1 ball each of #452 Purple Prelude (A), #149 Periwinkle Heather (B), #453 Rust Roadster (C) and #1308 Beach Berry (D)
> › Size J/10 (6mm) crochet hook or size needed to obtain gauge
> › Yarn needle

GAUGE

> › 14 sts and 9 rows in scarf pattern = 4" (10.2cm)
> › Motif = 4¾" (12.1cm) square
> › Take time to check gauge

Motifs (make 2)

With D, ch 4; join with sl st to form a ring.

Round 1: Beg-cl in ring, [ch 3, cl] 7 times in ring, ch 3, join with sl st in top of 1st cl (8 cl; 8 ch-3 sps). Fasten off D.

Round 2: With RS facing, join C with a sc in any cl, *3 sc in next ch-3 sp, sc in next cl; rep from * around, 3 sc in last ch-3 sp; join with sl st in 1st sc (32 sc). Fasten off C.

Round 3: With RS facing, join B with sl st in blps only of any sc, ch 3 (counts as 1st dc), dc in each of next 6 sts, 2 dc in next st, *dc in each of next 7 sts, 2 dc in next st; rep from * around; join with sl st in top of beg ch-3 (36 dc). Fasten off B.

Round 4: With RS facing, join A with sc in any dc, sc in same st, sc in each of next 7 dc, 2 sc in next st; *ch 3, 2 sc in next st, sc in each of next 7 dc, 2 sc in next dc; rep from * around, ch 3; join with sl st in 1st sc (44 sc, 4 ch-3 sps).

Round 5: Ch 1, sc in each sc across to next corner, (3 sc in next ch-3 sp), sc in each sc across to next corner; rep from * around; join with sl st in 1st sc (56 sc).

Assembly

With A and yarn needle, whipstitch one Motif to base of Row 1 of scarf. Whipstitch other Motif to top edge of Row 82.

Edging

Round 1 (RS):): With RS facing, starting in lower right corner of scarf, join A with sc in corner sc of Motif, 2 sc in same st, sc in each st across Motif, *sc evenly across length of the scarf, working 2 sc in each row-end dc, and 1 sc in each row-end sc*, [sc in each st across to corner of Motif, 3 sc in corner sc] twice, sc in each st across to beg of scarf; rep from * to * once; sc in each st across to corner of Motif, 3 sc in corner sc, sc in each st across to beg; join with a sl st in blp only of 1st sc. Do not fasten off.

Round 2: Working in blps only, *ch 2, sk next st, sl st in next st; rep from * around; join with sl st in 1st sl st. Fasten off.

SCARF STITCH DIAGRAM

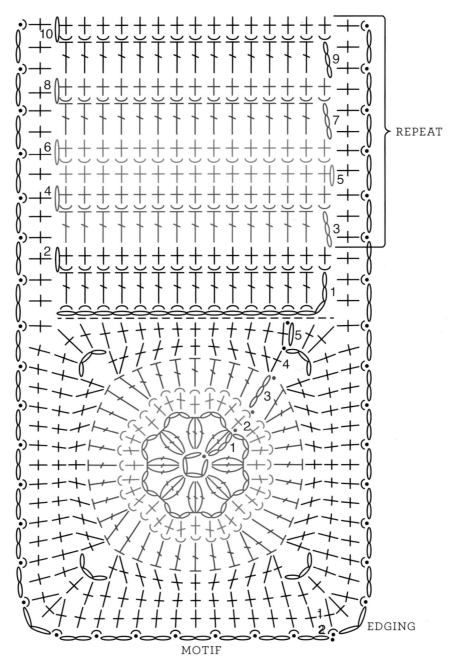

REPEAT

EDGING

MOTIF

Knockout Corsage

I'm a terrible gardener, but even I can grow these pretty flowers. Luckily, I have a lovely Knockout Rosebush in my yard that requires very little care and still provides lovely blooms. This permanent corsage is my version of a *Knockout*.

FINISHED SIZE
› 3½" (8.9cm) in diameter

MATERIALS
› Premier Primo Yarn (3.5 oz/273 yds/ 250m/100g per ball): 1 ball each #0001 White (A) and #0005 Peach (B)
› Size F/5 (3.75mm) crochet hook or size needed to obtain gauge
› Yarn needle
› 1 pin back

GAUGE
› Rounds 1–4 = 3½" (8.9cm) in diameter
› Take time to check gauge

PATTERN NOTES

All rounds are worked on the Right Side without turning.

Special stitches

Picot: Ch 3, hdc in 3rd ch from hook.

CORSAGE

With A, ch 4; join with sl st to form a ring.

Round 1: Ch 1, 8 sc in ring; join with sl st in 1st sc (8 sc).

Round 2: Ch 1, working in blps only, 2 sc in each sc around; join with sl st in 1st sc (16 sc).

Round 3: Ch 1, sc in same st, ch 7, sk next st; *sc in next st, ch 7, sk next st; rep from * around; join with sl st in 1st sc (8 sc, 8 ch-7 loops). Fasten off A.

Round 4: With RS facing, working behind the ch-7 loops of Round 3 and into the skipped sts on Round 2, join B with sl st in any skipped sc of Round 3. Ch 4 (counts as tr), 4 more tr in same st, picot, *5 tr in next skipped sc, picot, rep from * around; join with sl st in top beg ch-4 (40 tr, 8 picot). Fasten off B.

Round 5: With RS facing, working rem lps of sts in Round 1, join A with sc in any sc in Round 1 (hdc, dc) in same st, *(dc, hdc, sc) in next sc, (sc, hdc, dc) in next sc; rep from * 3 times; (dc, hdc, sc) in last sc; join with sl st in 1st sc (8 dc, 8 hdc, 8 sc). Fasten off.

Finishing

Weave in ends. With yarn and yarn needle, sew pin back onto back of flower or glue it on.

STITCH DIAGRAM 1

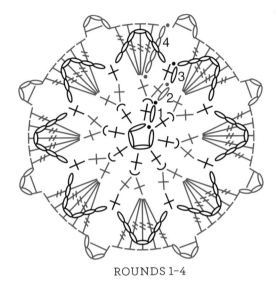

ROUNDS 1–4

STITCH DIAGRAM 2

ROUND 5

Mouse Baby Set

There is nothing more motivating than a newborn to make you want to get out your hooks! This adorable set is high on Awww factor but quick enough that it's not a major commitment. In this set, you are practicing your increasing and decreasing skills. The ears and tail are an introduction to the bits and pieces used in amigurumi crochet.

FINISHED SIZE
› Newborn 12" (30.5cm) hat; hat is 5¼" (13.3cm) crown to brim

MATERIALS
› Plymouth Encore (3.5 oz/200 yds/ 183m/ 100g per ball): 1 ball #1415 Fawn Mix (A)
› Plymouth Encore Tweed (3.5 oz/200 yds/ 183m/100g per ball): 1 ball #1363 Oatmeal (B)
› Size I/9 (5.5mm) crochet hook or size needed to obtain gauge
› Yarn needle

GAUGE
› 15 sts = 4" (10.2cm); 7 rows dc = 3½" (8.9cm)
› Take time to check gauge

PATTERN NOTES

› Rows on the hat are joined but not turned.

› Rows on the diaper cover are turned.

› Beginning ch-2 counts as first double crochet.

› Beginnng ch-2 on ears count as first half double crochet.

Special Stitches

Double crochet decrease 2 together (dc2tog): [Yo, insert hook in next st, yo, draw yarn through sp, yo, draw through 2 lps on hook] twice, yo, draw yarn through 3 lps on hook.

Back post double crochet (BPdc): Yo, insert hook from back to front to back again around the post of designated st, yo, draw yarn through st, [yo, draw yarn through 2 lps on hook] twice.

Front post double crochet (FPdc): Yo, insert hook from front to back to front again around the post of designated st, yo, draw yarn through st, [yo, draw yarn through 2 lps on hook] twice.

HAT

With A, ch 4, join with sl st in 1st ch to form a ring.

Row 1 (RS): Ch 2 (counts as dc here and throughout), 7 dc in ring; join with sl st in top of beg ch-2 (8 dc).

Row 2: Ch 2, dc in same st, 2 dc in each st around; join with sl st in top of beg ch-2 (16 dc).

Row 3: Ch 2, 2 dc in next st, *dc in next st, 2 dc in next st; rep from * around; join with sl st in top of beg ch-2 (24 dc).

Row 4: Ch 2, dc in next st, *2 dc in next st**, dc in each of next 2 sts; rep from * around, ending last rep at **; join with sl st in top of beg ch-2 (32 dc).

Row 5: Ch 2, dc in each of next 2 sts, *2 dc in next st**, dc in each of next 3 sts; rep from * around, ending last rep at **; join with sl st in top of beg ch-2 (40 dc).

Row 6: Ch 2, dc in each of next 3 sts, *2 dc in next st**, dc in each of next 4 sts; rep from * around, ending last rep at **; join with sl st in top of beg ch-2 (48 dc).

Rows 7–9: Ch 2, dc in each st around; join with sl st in top of beg ch-2 (48 dc).

Row 10: Ch 2, [BPdc around next st, FPdc around next st] 23 times to last st, BPdc in last st (48 sts).

Row 11: Ch 2, *BPdc around the post of next BPdc **, FPdc around the post of next FPdc; rep from * around, ending last rep at **, BPdc in last BPdc; join with sl st in top of beg ch-2. Fasten off A.

EARS (MAKE 2)

With B, ch 3; join with sl st in 1st ch to form a ring.

Row 1 (RS): Ch 2 (counts as hdc here and throughout Ear), 3 hdc in ring, turn (4 hdc).

Row 2 (WS): Ch 2, hdc in 1st st, hdc in each of next 2 sts, 2 hdc in last st, turn (6 hdc).

Row 3: Ch 2, hdc in each st across, turn (6 hdc).

Row 4: Ch 3 (counts as dc), [dc2tog over next 2 sts] twice, hdc in last st (3 dc, 1 hdc). Fasten off B.

Ears Edging

Round 1: With RS facing, join A with sc in ch-3 ring below row 1 of ear, sc in same ring, work 14 sc evenly spaced around outer edge of ear, sc in ch-3 ring; join with sl st in 1st sc (17 sc). *Note:* Ear will begin to cup toward the front.

Round 2: Ch 1, 2 sc in each st around; join with sl st in 1st sc. Fasten off A, leaving 6" (15.2cm) sewing length (34 sc).

Rep Rounds 1 and 2 for 2nd ear.

With yarn needle and sewing lengths, sew Ears to Hat as pictured.

EARS STITCH DIAGRAM

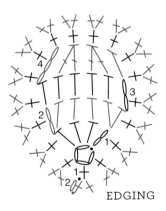

EDGING

DIAPER COVER

With A, ch 24.

Row 1 (RS): Dc in 4th ch from hook, dc in each ch across, turn (22 dc).

Rows 2–4: Ch 2 (counts as dc here and throughout), dc in each st across, turn (22 dc).

Row 5: Ch 2 [dc2tog over next 2 sts] twice, dc in each st across to last 5 sts, [dc2tog over next 2 sts] twice, dc in last st, turn (18 sts).

Row 6: Rep Row 5 (14 sts).

Rows 7–14: Ch 2, dc in each st, turn (14 dc).

Row 15: Ch 2, 2 dc in each of next 2 st, dc in each st across to last 3 sts, 2 dc in each of next 2 st, dc in last st, turn (18 sts).

Row 16: Rep Row 15 (22 sts).

Rows 17–20: Ch 2, dc in each st across, turn. Fasten off A (22 sts).

Finishing

Fold Diaper Cover in half with RS facing each other, so that Row 1 matches with Row 20 at top edge. With A and tapestry needle, working down from top, match row-end sts and sew side seams for 5 rows. Rep on other side. Turn Cover RS out.

Leg Openings

With RS facing, join A with sc in any st of 1 leg opening, ch 1, work 17 sc evenly spaced around opening; join with sl st in 1st sc. Fasten off (18 sc). Rep Leg Trim around other leg opening.

Waist Band

Round 1 (RS): With RS facing, join A with sl st in 1st dc on top edge, to left of side seam, ch 2, *BPdc around post of next st**, FPdc around post of next st; rep from * around, ending last rep at **; join with sl st in top of beg ch-2 (44 sts). Fasten off A.

TAIL

With A, ch 21.

Row 1: Sl st in 2nd ch from hook and in each of next 10 ch, sc in each of last 9 ch. Fasten off, leaving a sewing length. Using yarn needle and sewing length, sew Tail to back of Diaper Cover.

Finishing

Weave in ends.

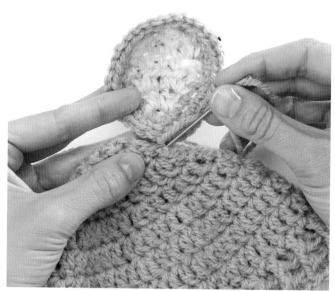

With yarn needle and yarn end, sew ears in place.

With yarn needle and yarn end, sew tail in place.

DIAPER STITCH DIAGRAM

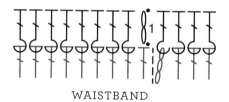

WAISTBAND

DIAPER COVER

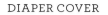
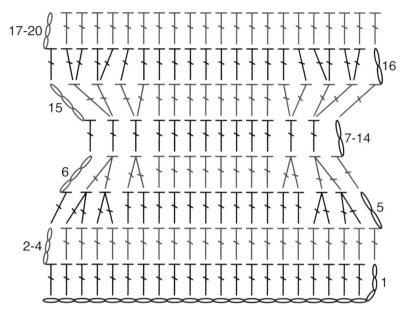

HAT STITCH DIAGRAM

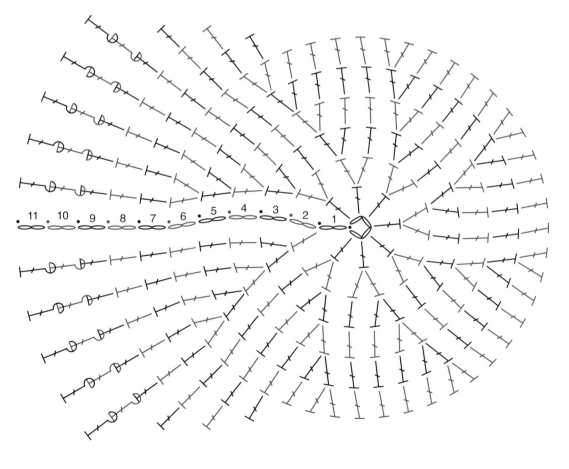

FINISHED SIZE
› 8¼" (21cm) × 8" (20.3cm)

MATERIALS
› Peaches & Creme (2.5 oz/120 yds/110m/ 70.9g per ball): 1 ball each of #01730 Bright Aqua (A) and #01712 Bright Lime (B)
› Size I/9 (5.5mm) crochet hook or size needed to obtain gauge
› Yarn needle

GAUGE
› 23 sts = 7" (17.8cm); 15 rows in pattern = 6½" (16.5cm)
› Take time to check gauge

Pergola Dishcloth

I just love the sound of the word *pergola*. The pergola is a lattice-type structure built in gardens to provide space for vines and foliage to grow and create shade. Just like climbing vines, the post stitches in this dish-cloth will teach you to create winding, textured cables.

PATTERN NOTES

Always skip a stitch in the current row behind each post stitch made.

Special Stitches

Back post double crochet (BPdc): Yo, insert hook from back to front to back again around the post of designated st, yo, draw yarn through st, [yo, draw yarn through 2 lps on hook] twice.

Front post double crochet (FPdc): Yo, insert hook from front to back to front again around the post of designated st, yo, draw yarn through st, [yo, draw yarn through 2 lps on hook] twice.

Front post treble crochet (FPtr): Yo (twice), insert hook from front to back to front again around the post of designated st, yo, draw yarn through st, [yo, draw yarn through 2 lps on hook] 3 times.

DISHCLOTH

With A, ch 25.

Row 1 (WS): Dc in 4th ch from hook, dc in each ch across, turn (23 dc).

Row 2 (RS): Ch 2 (counts as hdc here and throughout), *FPdc around the post of next dc, hdc in next st; rep from * across, turn.

Row 3: Ch 3 (counts as dc here and throughout), dc in each st across, turn.

Row 4: Ch 2, sk next 2 sts, *FPtr around the post of next FPdc 2 rows below, hdc in next st on current row, FPtr around the post of last skipped FPdc 2 rows below, (X made), hdc in next st in current row*; rep from * to * once, [FPtr around the post of next FPdc 2 rows below, hdc in next st] 3 times, rep from * to * twice, turn.

Row 5: Rep Row 3.

Row 6: Ch 2, *FPtr around the post of next FPtr 2 rows below, hdc in next st in current row; rep from * across, turn.

Row 7: Rep Row 3.

Row 8: Ch 2 (counts as hdc here and throughout), **FPtr around the post of next FPtr 2 rows below, hdc in next st in current row, *FPtr around the post of next FPdc 2 rows below, hdc in next st on current row, FPtr around the post of last skipped FPdc 2 rows below, hdc in next st*; rep from * to * once; rep from ** once, FPtr around the post of next FPtr 2 rows below, hdc in next st in current row, turn.

Row 9: Rep Row 3.

Row 10: Rep Row 6.

Row 11: Rep Row 3.

Row 12: Ch 2, sk next 2 sts, *FPtr around the post of next FPtr 2 rows below, sk 1 st on current row, hdc in next st on current row, FPtr around the post of last skipped FPtr 2 rows below, sk 1 st on current row (X made), hdc in next st*; rep from * to * once, [hdc in next FPtr around next FPtr 2 rows below, sk next st in current row, hdc in next st] 3 times, rep from * to * twice, turn.

Row 13: Rep Row 3.

Row 14: Rep Row 6.

Row 15: Ch 2, turn, *BPdc around the post of next st, hdc in next st; rep from * across, turn. Do not fasten off.

Edging

Round 1: With A, ch 1, sc in each st across, ch 3, working in row-end sts on side edge, work 23 sc evenly spaced across, ch 3, working across opposite side of foundation ch, sc in each ch across, ch 3, working in row-end sts on side edge, work 23 sc evenly spaced across, ch 3; join with sl st in 1st sc. Fasten off A, join B.

Round 2: With B, ch 1, *sc in each st across, 3 sc in ch-3 corner sp; rep from * around; join with sl st in 1st sc. Fasten off B.

Round 3: Join A with sl st in any st, sl st in each st around; join with sl st in 1st sl st. Fasten off. Weave in ends.

HOW TO CROCHET CABLES

1. Front post treble crochet begins with two yarn overs.

2. Insert the hook from the front to the back to the front and grab the yarn.

3. Pull the working yarn along as you back the hook out from the post of the stitch. Complete the stitch with a yarn over and pull through two loops on the hook twice.

4. Treble crochet in the next stitch.

5. The hook shows where the next front post treble crochet will be worked.

6. Work the next front post treble crochet in the indicated previous stitch.

7. One X is made of crossed front post treble crochet stitches.

DISHCLOTH STITCH DIAGRAM

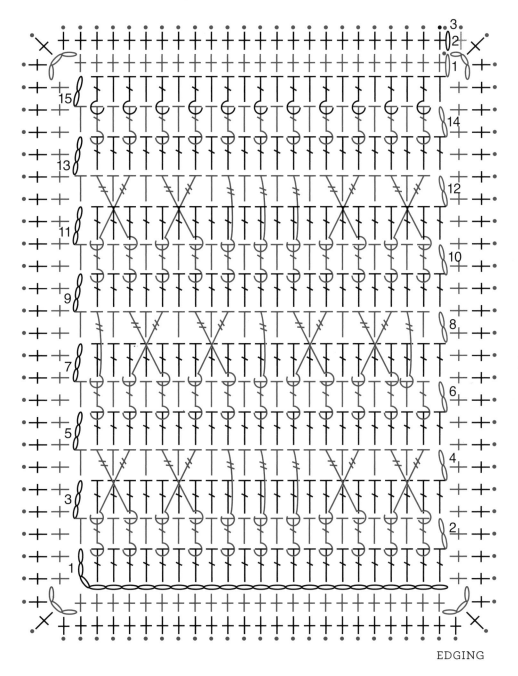

EDGING

FINISHED SIZE

› 7¾" (19.7cm)

› Add length in 1½" (3.8cm) increments by adding more motifs

MATERIALS

› Premier Deborah Norville Serenity Sock yarn (1.76 oz/230 yds/210m/50g per ball): 1 skein #5004 Purple

› Sizes E/4 (3.5mm) crochet hook or size needed to obtain gauge

› Yarn needle

› Magnetic barrel clasp

GAUGE

› First two rounds of Motif = 1½" (3.8cm) diameter

› Take time to check gauge

Memory Bracelet

The Memory Bracelet is an easy gift you can knock out in twenty minutes. Every time the recipient looks at it, she will remember you. I love the idea of using a bracelet to remind myself of something I want to remember. Make the join-as-you-go motifs in different colors to remind you of different things!

PATTERN NOTES

The first motif is made separately, then subsequent motifs are joined to the first as they are worked.

Special Stitches

Adjustable ring: Wrap thread in a ring around the index finger, ending with thread tail behind the working thread. Remove from finger and grip the ring and tail firmly between middle finger and thumb. Insert hook through center of ring; with working thread, yo, draw up lp, work sts of 1st Round in ring. After the 1st Round of sts has been completed, pull gently but firmly on thread tail to close ring.

Beginning Cluster (beg-cl): Ch 3, [yo, insert hook in same sp, yo, draw up a lp, yo, draw through 2 lps on hook] twice, yo, draw through 3 lps on hook.

Cluster (cl): [Yo, insert hook in sp, yo, draw up a lp, yo, draw through 2 lps on hook] 3 times in same sp, yo, draw through 4 lps on hook.

BRACELET MOTIF STITCH DIAGRAMS

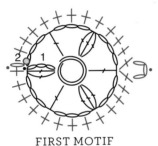

FIRST MOTIF

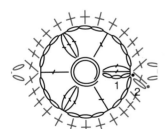

SECOND MOTIF

LAST MOTIF

FIRST MOTIF

Thread half of magnetic barrel clasp on yarn and push it several inches down the length of the yarn. Make adjustable ring.

Round 1 (RS): Work beg-cl in ring, [ch 3, dc in ring, ch 3, cl in ring] twice, ch 3, dc in ring, ch 3, push clasp half up to hook; join with sl st in beg-cl.

Round 2: Ch 1, sc in 1st cl, 3 sc in next ch-3 sp, sc in next dc, 3 sc in next ch-3 sp, sc in next cl, 3 sc in next ch-3 sp, (sc, ch 3, sc) in next dc, 3 sc in next ch-3 sp, sc in cl, 3 sc in next ch-3 sp, sc in next dc, 3 sc in next ch-3 sp; join with sl st in 1st sc. Fasten off.

CENTER MOTIFS (2 AND 3)

Round 1: Work beg-cl in ring, [ch 3, dc in ring, ch 3, cl in ring] twice, ch 3, dc in ring; join with sl st in 1st beg-cl.

Round 2: Ch 1, (sc, ch 3, sc) in 1st cl, *3 sc in next ch-3 sp, sc in next dc, 3 sc in next ch-3 sp, sc in next cl, 3 sc in next ch-3 sp, (sc, ch 1, sl st in ch-3 lp of previous motif, ch 1, sc) in next dc, 3 sc in next ch-3 sp, sc in next cl, 3 sc in next ch-3 sp, sc in next dc, 3 sc in next ch-3 sp; join with sl st in 1st sc. Fasten off.

Note: For added length, work additional motifs here.

FINAL MOTIF

Thread second half of magnetic barrel clasp on yarn and push it several inches down the length of the yarn. Make adjustable ring.

Round 1: Work beg-cl in ring, [ch 3, dc in ring, ch 3, cl in ring] twice, ch 3, dc in ring, ch 3, push clasp half up to the hook; join with sl st in 1st beg-cl.

Round 2: Ch 1, (sc, ch 3, sc) in 1st cl, *3 sc in next ch-3 sp, sc in next dc, 3 sc in next ch-3 sp, sc in next cl, 3 sc in next ch-3 sp, (sc, ch 1, sl st in ch-3 lp of previous motif, ch 1, sc) in next dc, 3 sc in next ch-3 sp, sc in next cl, 3 sc in next ch-3 sp, sc in next dc, 3 sc in next ch-3 sp; join with sl st in 1st sc. Fasten off. Weave in ends.

> ### DESIGNER TIP
>
> You can find magnetic barrel clasps in the jewelry department of your local craft store.
>
> Experiment with different yarns and threads. Hold two strands of contrasting yarns together for a larger bracelet with a more Bohemian look.

Pentagon Cowl

Two rows of mirrored pentagon motifs create dimensionality and volume in this easy join-as-you-go cowl. One row has a tight final edging while the other has a flared final edging to create an hourglass shape.

FINISHED SIZE

› 16" (40.6cm) wide when flat; 11" (27.9cm) deep. Center seam is 13" (33cm) across when folded and joined; 26" (66cm) in circumference.

MATERIALS

› Berroco Weekend (3.5 oz/205 yds/187m/ 100g per ball): 1 hank each of #5926 Clothesline (A), #5910 Cornsilk (B) and #5947 Blood Orange (C)

› Size I/9 (5.5mm) crochet hook or size needed to obtain gauge

› Yarn needle

GAUGE

› One motif = 5" (12.7cm) from one point to opposite side

› Take time to check gauge

PATTERN NOTES

› Beginning ch-3 counts as a double crochet.

› Beginning ch-2 counts as a half double crochet.

› All rounds are worked on the Right Side without turning.

Special Stitches

Beginning 4-tr cluster (Beg 4-tr cl) (worked over 2 sts): Ch 4, yo (twice), insert hook in same st, yo, draw yarn through st, [yo, draw through 2 lps on hook] twice, *yo (twice), insert hook in next st, yo, draw yarn through st, [yo, draw through 2 lps on hook] twice; rep from * once in same st, yo, draw yarn through all lps on hook.

4-tr cluster (4-tr cl) (worked over 2 stitches): *Yo (twice), insert hook in next st, yo, draw yarn through st, [yo, draw through 2 lps on hook] twice*; rep from * once in same st; rep from * to * twice in next st, yo, draw yarn through 5 lps on hook.

FIRST MOTIF

With A, ch 5; join with sl st in 1st ch to form a ring.

Round 1: Ch 2 (counts as hdc), 9 hdc in ring; join with sl st in top of beg ch-2 (10 hdc).

Round 2: Beg 4-tr cl in 1st 2 sts, *ch 7, 4-tr cl worked in next 2 sts; rep from * 3 times, ch 7, join with sl st in top 1st 4-tr cl. Fasten off A.

Round 3: With RS facing, join B with dc in any ch-7 sp, 6 more dc in same sp, *sc in next 4-tr cl, 7 dc in next ch-7 sp; rep from * 3 times, sc in next 4-tr cl; join with sl st in 1st 4-tr cl. Fasten off B.

Round 4: With RS facing, join C with tr in any sc, (3 tr, ch 1, 4 tr) in same st, *sk next 3 dc, sc in next dc, sk next 3 dc, (4 tr, ch 1, 4 tr) in next sc; rep from * 3 times, sk next 3 dc, sc in next dc, sk next 3 dc; join with sl st in 1st tr. Fasten off C.

MOTIFS 2-14

Make and join 13 more Motifs following Assembly Diagram for placement. Work same as First Motif through Round 3.

Round 4 (joining on one side): With RS facing, join C with tr in any sc, (3 tr, ch 1, 4 tr) in same st, [sk next 3 dc, sc in next dc, sk next 3 dc, (4 tr, ch 1, 4 tr) in next sc] twice, [sk next 3 dc, sc in next dc, sk next 3 dc, (4 tr, sl st in corresponding ch-1 sp on previous Motif, 4 tr) in next sc] twice, sk next 3 dc, sc in next dc, sk next 3 dc; join with sl st in 1st tr. Fasten off C.

Round 4 (joining on 2 sides): With RS facing, join C with tr in any sc, (3 tr, ch 1, 4 tr) in same st, sk next 3 dc, sc in next dc, sk next 3 dc, (4 tr, ch 1, 4 tr) in next sc] twice, [sk next 3 dc, sc in next dc, sk next 3 dc, (4 tr, sl st in corresponding ch-1 sp on previous Motif, 4 tr) in next sc] 3 times, sk next 3 dc, sc in next dc, sk next 3 dc; join with sl st in 1st tr. Fasten off C.

Round 4 (joining on 3 sides): With RS facing, join C with tr in any sc, (3 tr, ch 1, 4 tr) in same st, [sk next 3 dc, sc in next dc, sk next 3 dc, (4 tr, sl st in corresponding ch-1 sp on previous Motif, 4 tr) in next sc] 4 times, sk next 3 dc, sc in next dc, sk next 3 dc; join with sl st in 1st tr. Fasten off C.

First Edging (designed to draw in)

Row 1 (RS): With RS facing, join C with sl st in ch-1 sp of a middle point of a pentagon (one that is not joined), ch 3 (counts as dc), 6 dc in same ch-1 sp, *ch 2, sk next 4 tr, sc in next sc, ch 2, sk next 4 tr, dc2tog working over next 2 joined ch-1 sps, ch 2, sk next 4 tr, sc in next sc, ch 2, sk 4 tr**, 7 dc in next ch-1 sp; rep from * around, ending last rep at **; join with sl st in top beg ch-3. Fasten off.

Second Edging (designed to flare out)

Row 1 (RS): With RS facing, join C with sl st in ch-1 sp of a middle point of a pentagon (one that is not joined), ch 3 (counts as dc), 6 dc in same ch-1 sp, *ch 1, sk next 4 tr, 5 dc in next sc, ch 1, sk next 4 tr, dc2tog working over next 2 joined ch-1 sps, ch 1, sk next 4 tr, 5 dc in next sc, ch 1, sk next 4 tr**, 7 dc in next ch-1 sp; rep from * around, ending last rep at **; join with sl st in top beg ch-3. Fasten off.

Finishing

Weave in ends.

HOW TO JOIN MOTIFS

1. Place four treble crochet in the corner space and insert the hook into the chain-one space of an adjacent motif to be joined.

2. Slip stitch in the corresponding corner.

3. When joining to a pair that have already been joined, insert the hook into the slip stitch where the two come together.

4. Complete the round on the current motif.

5. A fourth motif will fit in the wedge of white space in the photo. The piece will have dimension and will not lie flat because of the nature of pentagons.

ASSEMBLY DIAGRAM

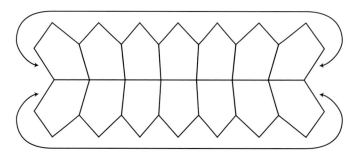

MOTIF STITCH DIAGRAM

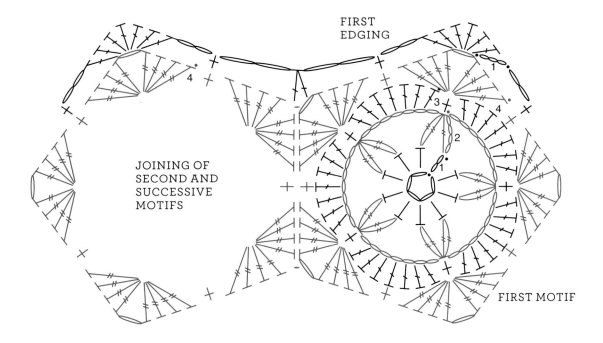

FIRST
EDGING

JOINING OF
SECOND AND
SUCCESSIVE
MOTIFS

FIRST MOTIF

EDGING STITCH DIAGRAM

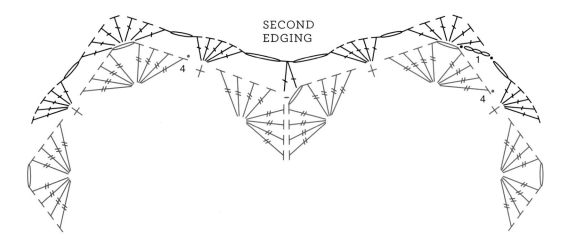

SECOND
EDGING

All Shook Up

Lacy stitch patterns are one of the keys to making projects in a flash. This triangular shawl is deceptive. It looks like a big project, but since it's narrower at the ends, it's really not as big as it looks. This deception leads to instant gratification. Some crocheters are intimidated by increases and decreases in a stitch pattern. You'll practice those skills here in this intermediate shawlette.

PATTERN NOTES

Special Stitches

Shell (sh): [(tr, ch 1) twice, tr] in same st.

Picot: Ch 5, 2 tr in 5th ch from hook.

Treble crochet 2 together (tr2tog): *Yo (twice), insert hook in next st, yo, draw yarn through st, yo, draw yarn through 2 lps on hook] twice; rep from * once, yo, draw yarn through 3 lps on hook.

SHAWLETTE

Increase every other even row: 4, 8, 12, 16, etc.

Row 1 (WS): Ch 6 (counts as tr, ch 1), (tr, ch 1, tr) in 6th ch from hook, turn (1 sh).

Row 2: Work picot, sh in 1st tr, sk next (ch-1 sp, tr, ch-1 sp), tr in last tr, turn (1 sh).

Row 3: Ch 4 (counts as tr here and throughout), *sh in middle tr of each sh across to center of last sh, sk next ch-1 sp, tr in last tr, turn (do not work in picot) (1 sh).

Row 4 (inc): Work picot, sh in 1st tr, sh in middle tr of each sh across to last 3 sts, sk next (ch-1 sp, tr), tr in last tr, turn (2 sh).

Row 5: Rep Row 3 (2 sh).

Row 6 (no inc): Work picot, sk next (2 tr, ch-1 sp), *sh in middle tr of each sh across to last 3 sts, sk next (ch-1 sp, tr), tr in last tr, turn (2 sh).

Row 7: Rep Row 3 (2 sh).

Row 8 (inc): Rep Row 4 (3 sh).

Rows 9–32: Rep Rows 5–8 (6 times) (9 sh at end of last row).

Note: Row 32 is the deepest point of the shawlette.

Begin Decreasing

Row 33 (dec): Ch 4, sk next (tr, ch-1 sp), sh in middle tr of each sh across to last 2 sh, sh in 2nd to last sh, sk next (3 ch-1 sps), tr in last tr of last sh, turn (8 sh).

Row 34: Rep Row 6.

FINISHED SIZE
› 65" (165cm) wide; 12½" (31.8cm) deep (at Row 32)

MATERIALS
› Drew Emborsky Decades Iconic (4 oz/ 250 yds/229m/113g per ball): 1 hank 1950s Blue Suede Shoes
› Size J/10 (6mm) crochet hook or size needed to obtain gauge
› Yarn needle

GAUGE
› 3 reps = 4" (10.2cm); 15 sts in pattern and 4 rows in pattern = 4" (10.2cm)
› Take time to check gauge

HOW TO MAKE AN EDGING WHILE WORKING THE BODY

1. Edge picots are added after completing an odd numbered row.

2. Place the picot in the first st of the new row. Chain five and make two picot in the fifth chain from the hook.

3. The picot will hang off the edge.

SHAWL STITCH DIAGRAM

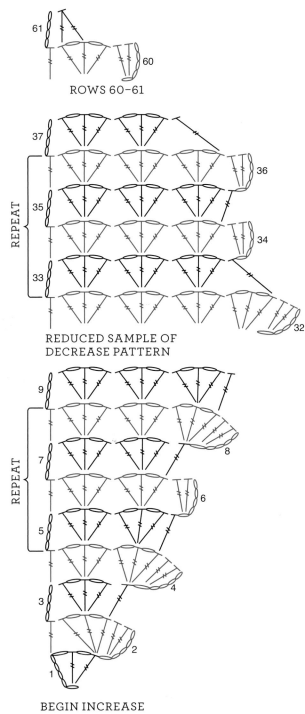

ROWS 60–61

REDUCED SAMPLE OF
DECREASE PATTERN

BEGIN INCREASE
PATTERN

Cosmic Hexagon Tote

Let your color compulsion go wild with this fun tote. Use up stash scrap colors for a multicolor explosion. I'm going to use mine as a project tote. You may have learned join-as-you-go motifs in the earlier projects. Now you'll practice crocheting motifs together. It creates a fabric that is denser, which is better for holding your crochet projects. While whipstitching motifs together is the traditional method, crocheting them together in this pattern is fun, and you get to do more of what you love . . . crochet!

PATTERN NOTES

Motif Rounds are worked on the Right Side without turning. Join rounds with a slip stitch unless otherwise indicated. (Make 4 of color scheme A and 3 of color scheme B.)

Color scheme A (make 4)
> › Round 1 A
> › Round 2 B
> › Round 3 C
> › Round 4 A
> › Round 5 C
> › Round 6 B

Color Scheme B (make 3)
> › Round 1 B
> › Round 2 C
> › Round 3 A
> › Round 4 B
> › Round 5 A
> › Round 6 C

TOTE

Motif (make 7)

With Round 1 color, ch 5; join with sl st in 1st ch to form a ring.

Round 1: Ch 3 (counts as dc), 17 dc in same ring; join with sl st in top of beg ch-3 (18 dc). Fasten off.

FINISHED SIZE
> › 7¾" × 12" (19.7cm × 30.5cm) when flat
> › 11" (27.9cm) tall when standing
> › Strap: 1" (2.5cm) × 18" (45.7cm) (4 rows)
> › One motif: 5¼" (13.3cm) side to side
> › One motif: 6" (15.2cm) point to point

MATERIALS
> › Classic Elite Yarns, Color By Kristin (1.76 oz/93 yds/85m/ 50g per ball): 1 ball each of #3248 Deep Blue Sea (A), #3232 Raspberry (B) and #3236 Mushroom (C)
> › Size I/9 (5.5mm) crochet hook or size needed to obtain gauge
> › Yarn needle

GAUGE
> › First 6 rounds of Motif = 5¼" (13.3cm) (side to side) or 6" (15.2cm) (point to point)
> › Take time to check gauge

Round 2: With RS facing, join Round 2 color with sl st in any st, sl st in each st around; join with sl st in 1st sl st (36 sl sts). Fasten off.

Round 3: Working in Round 1 lps behind Round 2 sl sts, with RS facing, join Round 3 color with sc in any st in Round 1, sc in same st, 2 sc in each dc around; join with sl st in 1st sc. Fasten off.

Round 4: With RS facing, join Round 4 color with tr in any st, tr in same st, *tr in each of next 5 sts**, 2 tr in next st; rep from * around, ending last rep at **; join with sl st in top 1st tr (42 tr). Fasten off.

Round 5: With RS facing, join Round 5 color with dc in any st, 2 more dc in same st, *hdc in next st, sc in each of next 4 sts, hdc in next st**, 3 dc in next st; rep from * around, ending last rep at **; join with sl st in 1st dc (54 sts). Fasten off.

Round 6: With RS facing, join Round 6 color with sc in middle dc of any corner, 2 more sc in same st, sc in each st to next corner, *3 sc in middle dc of corner, sc in each st to next corner; rep from * around; join with sl st in 1st sc. Fasten off.

Assembly

With A, sc the motifs together with the RS facing each other and matching sts in blps only. See placement diagram. Sc the 3 B motifs together in a strip. Sc 3 of the 4 A motifs together in a strip. Sc the bottom of the A strip to the top of the B strip as shown in the diagram. Match the top Row B motif first and last to make a tube. Match the bottom Row A motif 1st and last to form a tube. The base is the 4th motif of color scheme A. All 6 sides of this base motif will be crocheted to all bottom sides of the 3 A motifs.

Top Edging

Round 1: With RS facing, starting in junction between 2 motifs at corner sc on top edge of Tote, working through both lps of sts, join A with sc2tog working 1st leg of st in corner on right side of junction, work 2nd leg in next corner st on left side of junction, complete sc2tog, *sc in each st across to center sc at point of Motif, 3 sc in center

sc of point, sc in each st across to next junction, ** sc2tog worked over 2 joined corner sc; rep from * around, ending last rep at **; join with sl st in 1st sc (72 sc). Do not fasten off.

Round 2: Ch 5 (counts as dtr), dtr in each of next 2 sts, *tr in each of next 3 sts, dc in each of next 3 sts, hdc in next st, sc in each of next 5 sts, hdc in next st, dc in each of next 3 sts, tr in each of next 3 sts**, dtr in each of next 5 sts; rep from * around, ending last rep at **, dtr in each of last 2 sts; join with sl st in top beg ch-5 (72 sts).

Rounds 3–4: Ch 1, sc in each st around; join with sl st in 1st sc (72 sc). Fasten off.

STRAP

With B, ch 71.

Row 1: Sc in 2nd ch from hook and in each ch across, turn (70 sc).

Row 2: Ch 1, sc in each st across, turn. Fasten off B.

Row 3: With RS facing, join A with sc in 1st st, sc in each st across, turn. Fasten off leaving a long sewing length.

Row 4: Working across opposite side of foundation ch, with RS facing, join A with sc in 1st ch, sc in each ch across. Fasten off, leaving a long sewing length.

With yarn needle, and using tails, sew strap on opposite edges of bag, approximately 36 sts apart.

Finishing

Weave in ends.

TOTE STITCH DIAGRAM

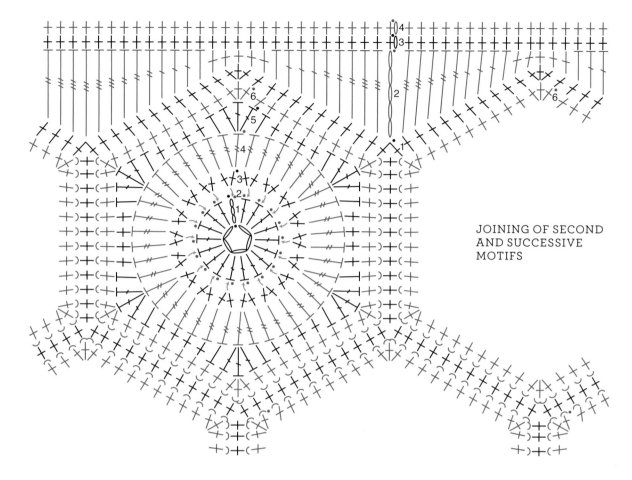

JOINING OF SECOND
AND SUCCESSIVE
MOTIFS

ASSEMBLY DIAGRAM

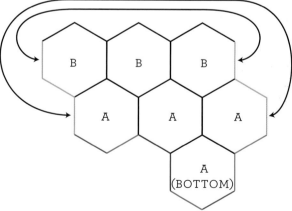

Honeysuckle Beret

I didn't name this project honeysuckle just because of the yarn color. The perfume of honeysuckle is strong in southern Ohio in summer, and it's one of the few flowers I can pick out by scent. Honeysuckle is eternal . . . it was present in my childhood and is common in my present.

PATTERN NOTES
All rounds are worked on the Right Side without turning. Rounds are joined with a slip stitch.

Special Stitches
Cluster (cl): [Yo, insert hook in sp, yo, draw up a lp, yo, draw through 2 lps on hook] 3 times in same sp, yo and pull through 4 lps on hook.

V stitch (V-st): (Dc, ch 2, dc) in same st.

HAT
Ch 5; join with sl st in 1st ch to form a ring.

Round 1 (RS): Ch 3, (counts as dc here and throughout), 11 dc in ring; join with sl st in top of beg ch-3 (12 dc).

Round 2: Ch 4 (counts as dc, ch 1), *cl in next st, ch 1**, dc in next st, ch 1; rep from * around, ending last rep at **; join with sl st in 3rd ch of beg ch-4 (6 dc; 6 cl; 12 ch-1 sps).

Round 3: Ch 5 (counts as dc, ch 2 here and throughout), dc in same st (counts as the beg V-st), *ch 2, cl in next cl, ch 2**, V-st in next dc; rep from * around, ending last rep at **; join with sl st in 3rd ch of beg ch-5 (6 cl; 6 V-sts).

Round 4: Ch 4, *cl in next ch-2 sp, ch 1, dc in next dc, ch 2, cl in next cl, ch 2**, dc in next dc, ch 1; rep from * around, ending last rep at **; join with sl st in 3rd ch of beg ch-4 (12 cl; 12 dc).

Round 5: Ch 5, *cl in next cl, ch 2**, dc in next dc, ch 2; rep from * around, ending last rep at **; join with sl st in 3rd ch of beg ch-5 (12 cl; 12 dc).

Round 6: Ch 5 (counts as dc, ch 2 here and throughout), dc in same st (counts as the beg V-st), *ch 1, cl in next cl, ch 1**, V-st in next dc; rep from * around, ending last rep at **; join with sl st in 3rd ch of beg ch-5 (12 cl; 12 V-sts).

Rounds 7–9: Rep Rounds 4–6 (48 cl; 48 dc at end of last round).

Round 10: Rep Round 4. Fasten off, leaving a long sewing length.

SKILL LEVEL

FINISHED SIZE
› 21" (53.3cm) in circumference

MATERIALS
› Universal Yarn Deluxe Worsted Superwash (3.5 oz/220 yds/201m/ 100g per ball): 1 ball #721 Honeysuckle

› Size I/9 (5.5mm) crochet hook or size needed to obtain gauge

› Yarn needle

› Locking stitch markers

GAUGE
› First 3 rounds of hat = 4" (10.2cm) in diameter

› First 10 rounds of hat = 12¼" (31.1cm) in diameter (before brim)

› Take time to check gauge

BAND

Ch 5.

Row 1 (RS): Working in back ridge only of ch sts, sc in 2nd ch from hook and in each ch across, turn (4 sc).

Rows 2–72: Ch 1, sc in blps only of each sc across, turn (4 sc). Note: Work until Band measures 18" (45.7cm) long, knowing that it will stretch to fit 20"–21" (50.8–53.3cm). Fasten off, leaving a sewing length.

Assembly

Matching sts, without twisting Band, sew last row to foundation ch. With locking st markers, pin the band evenly in place around Round 10 of the Hat. With yarn needle and yarn, sew Band to Round 10.

Edging

Round 1: With RS facing, join yarn with sc in any st on side edge of Band, sc in each row-end st around; join with sl st in 1st sc (72 sc).

Round 2: Ch 1, working in blps only, sc in each sc around; join with sl st in 1st sc (72 sc). Fasten off.

Finishing

Weave in ends.

**BAND AND EDGING
STITCH DIAGRAM**

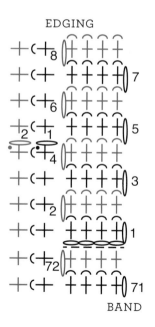

BERET STITCH DIAGRAM

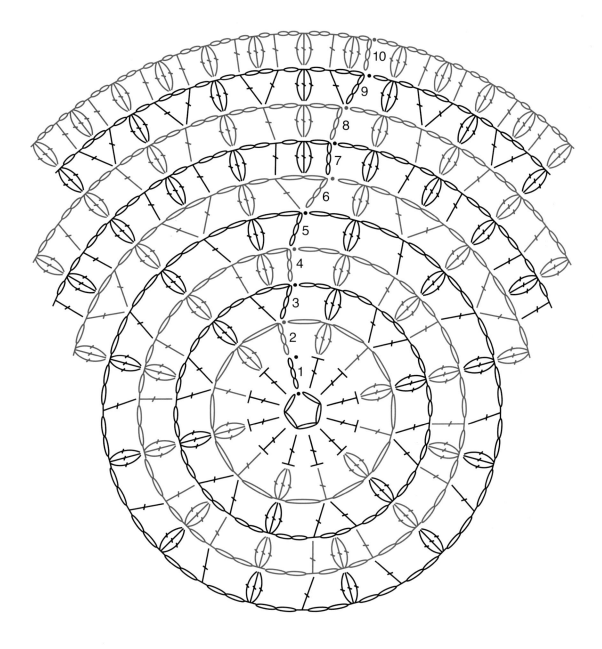

SKILL LEVEL

FINISHED SIZE

› 18" (45.7cm) in circum-ference (unstretched)

› Stretches to fit 21" (53.3cm) head

› 7" (17.8cm) deep from crown to edge of brim

MATERIALS

› Classic Elite Liberty Wool Print (1.76 oz/ 122 yds/112m/50g per ball): 2 balls #7825 Rose Explosion

› **Note:** *One ball was exactly enough yarn to make this hat at the gauge given. If your gauge is too big, you may use more and run out of yarn. This does not include yarn for swatching. So while the hat used only one ball, you may want to buy two.*

› Size I/9 (5.5mm) crochet hook or size needed to obtain gauge

› Yarn needle

GAUGE

› First two rnds of hat = 3" (7.6cm) in diameter

› First four rnds of hat = 6" (15.2cm) in diameter

› In cluster rnds, 7 rnds = 4" (10.2cm)

› Take time to check gauge

Delightful Hat

I was going to call this project the Happy Hat because I think I'd feel happy wearing it, but it sounded too silly. Then I remembered that my Mom used to call things that made her happy "delightful," and I thought that would do! You'll have the cluster stitch method down pat as you work this hat from the crown to the brim in a snug beanie style.

PATTERN NOTES

Rounds are joined but not turned. All rounds are worked on the Right Side.

Special Stitches

Beginning cluster (beg-cl): Ch 3, [yo, insert hook in same sp, yo, draw up a lp, yo, draw through 2 lps on hook] twice, yo, draw through 3 lps on hook.

Cluster (cl): [Yo, insert hook in sp, yo, draw up a lp, yo, draw through 2 lps on hook] 3 times in same sp, yo, draw through 4 lps on hook.

Beginning 3-tr cl (Beg 3-tr cl): Ch 4, *yo (twice), insert hook in same sp, yo, draw up a lp, [yo, draw through 2 lps on hook] twice; rep from * once, yo, draw through 3 lps on hook.

3-tr Cluster (3-tr cl): *Yo (twice), insert hook in next st, yo, draw yarn through st, [yo, draw through 2 lps on hook] twice*; rep from * 3 times in same st, yo, draw yarn through 4 lps on hook.

Picot: Ch 3, hdc in 3rd ch from hook.

HAT

Ch 4; join with sl st in 1st ch to form a ring.

Round 1: Ch 3 (counts as dc), 11 dc in ring; join with sl st in top of beg ch-3 (12 dc).

Round 2: Beg-cl in 1st st, ch 3, (cl, ch 3) in each dc around; join with sl st in 1st cl (12 cl).

Round 3: Ch 1, sc in 1st st, ch 5, (sc, ch 5) in each cl around; join with sl st in 1st sc (12 sc; 12 ch-5 sps).

Round 4: Sl st in next ch-5 sp, (Beg 3-tr cl, ch 5, 3-tr cl) in same ch-5 sp, *ch 5, 3-tr cl in next ch-5 sp, ch 5**, (3-tr cl, ch 5, 3-tr cl) in next ch-5 sp; rep from * around, ending last rep at **; join with sl st in 1st cl (18 3-tr cl, 18 ch-5 sps).

Round 5: Sl st in next ch-5 sp, (beg-cl, ch 2, cl) in same ch-5 sp, (cl, ch 2, cl) in each ch-5 sp around; join with sl st in 1st cl (36 cl; 18 ch-2 sps).

Round 6: Beg-cl in 1st st, ch 1, sk next ch-2 sp, *cl in each of next 2 cl, ch 1, sk next ch-2 sp; rep from * 16 times, cl in last cl; join with sl st in top of 1st cl (36 cl; 18 ch-1 sps).

Rounds 7–12: Beg-cl in 1st st, ch 1, sk ch-1 sp, *cl in each of next 2 cl, ch 1, sk next ch-1 sp; rep from * 16 times; cl in last cl; join with sl st in 1st cl (cl; 18 ch-1 sps).

Round 13: Sl st in next ch-1 sp, *picot, sk 2 cl, sl st in next ch-1 sp; rep from * around; ending with last sl st in 1st sl st. Fasten off. Weave in ends.

HAT STITCH DIAGRAM

FINISHED SIZE
- › 7" (17.8cm) long without clasp
- › 7½" (19.1cm) in circumference with clasp
- › 1" (2.5cm) wide

MATERIALS
- › Patons Grace (1.75 oz/136 yds/124m/ 50g per skein): 1 skein #62246 Leaf
- › Size E/4 (3.5mm) crochet hook or size needed to obtain gauge
- › Sewing needle and 12" (30.5cm) length of sewing thread or twisted wire beading needle
- › Seed beads. Sample uses 70 Delica® glass seed beads, opaque metallic luster, #11 round, DB27 Forest Green. Sold per pkg of 7.5g (.26 oz). Available at www.firemountain-gems.com/itemdetails/ H20DB0027V
- › Magnetic barrel clasp
- › Yarn needle

GAUGE
- › 35 sc = 7" (17.8cm); 2 rows in pattern = 1" (2.5cm)
- › Take time to check gauge

Cornelia Beaded Bracelet

Subtle beads, easy stitches and a convenient magnetic clasp make this bracelet a perfect gift to make multiple times. Our family visited the fantastic Biltmore Estate, which was opened in 1898. I can imagine the Vanderbilt daughter, Cornelia, wearing this vintage inspired beaded bracelet. Crocheting with beads is the skill you'll practice in this show-stopping accessory.

PATTERN NOTES

To customize length, take desired total length and subtract ½" (1.3cm) for clasp. Take the desired number of inches times the stitch gauge. Chain an even number of beginning chains.

Rows are worked on the Right Side without turning. Beads will show on the Wrong Side. On the finished bracelet, the beaded side is worn outward to show the beads.

Pre-string: Using a twisted wire beading needle, place the yarn through the eye of the beading needle, pass the beads from the wire needle onto the yarn; or place the 12" (30.5cm) length of sewing thread through the eye of the sewing needle. Double the thread and tie the ends together. Place 4" (10.2cm) of the yarn through the doubled sewing thread. Pass the beads onto the sewing needle, past the sewing thread and onto the working yarn.

Pre-string 70 beads (add a few extra in case of miscount or breakage). If you encounter a flawed bead while working, break it off and continue working. Add more than 70 beads for a longer bracelet. An additional 10 beads for each 1" (2.5cm) of added length.

Special Stitches

Bead ch (Bch): With slip knot on hook, slide bead up to hook, yo, draw through lp on hook for 1st Bch; slide bead up to hook, yo, draw through lp on hook.

Bead sc (Bsc) (Bead will appear on WS): Slide bead up to hook, insert hook in designated st or sp, yo, draw up a lp, yo, draw through 2 lps on hook.

BRACELET

Ch 36 (or an even number of chs for desired length; see Pattern Notes).

Row 1 (RS): Sc in 2nd ch from hook, and in each ch across (35 sc).

Row 2: Rotate and begin working across opposite side of foundation ch, Bsc in 1st ch, *ch 2, Bch, ch 2, sk next ch, Bsc in next ch; rep from * across.

Row 3: Rotate again and work in the sts of Row 1, ch 1, Bsc in each sc across. Fasten off leaving a 6" (15.2cm) tail.

Finishing

Thread half the magnetic barrel clasp onto the cut tail, pushing the clasp to the end of the row. Tie if desired or tightly weave in end. Cut a 10" (25.4cm) length of yarn. With yarn needle, sew the opposite end of the barrel clasp onto opposite end of bracelet. Weave in ends. Block.

BRACELET STITCH DIAGRAM

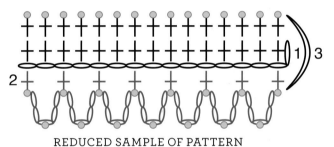

REDUCED SAMPLE OF PATTERN

HOW TO CROCHET WITH BEADS

1. To add a bead to a chain, bring the bead up toward the hook and grab the yarn on the far side of the bead.

2. Pull the working yarn through the loop on the hook to secure the bead.

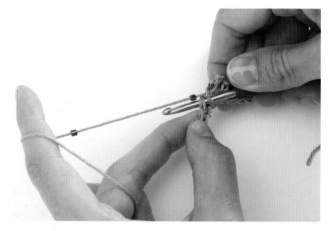

3. To add a bead to a single crochet, insert the hook in the next stitch and bring the bead up close to the work.

4. Yarn over on the far side of the bead.

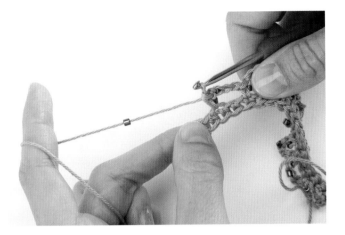

DESIGNER TIP

A large version of this project would make a lovely wedding garter.

5. Complete the single crochet by pulling through both loops on the hook.

Cabled Boot Cuffs

Stay warm, keep the snow out of your boots and be trendy all with one quick project. We take cabling to a new level by adding a simple surface slip stitch embellishment. The surface slip stitch can be added to any project to create lines, definition or a swath of color. Practice it here with chunky yarn and a big hook.

PATTERN NOTES

› Post stitches are worked into the double crochets two rows below, skipping the single crochet row.

› Cables are worked on the Right Side of the fabric.

› Single crochets are worked on the Wrong Side of the fabric in the cable portion.

Special Stitches

Front post double crochet (FPdc): Yo, insert hook from front to back to front again around the post of designated st, yo, draw yarn through st, [yo, draw yarn through 2 lps on hook] twice.

CUFF (MAKE 2)

With A, ch 16.

Row 1 (RS): Sc in 2nd ch from hook and in each of next 5 ch, ch 1, sk next ch, dc in each of next 6 ch, ch 1, sk next ch, dc in last ch, turn.

Row 2 (WS): Ch 1, sc in 1st dc, ch 1, sk next ch-1 sp, sc in each of next 6 sts, ch 1, sk next ch-1 sp, working in blps only, sc in each of last 6 sc, turn.

Row 3: Ch 1, sc in blps of 1st 6 sc, ch 1, sk next ch-1 sp, FPdc around the post of next dc 2 rows below, dc in next sc in current row, sk next dc, FPdc around the post of next dc, FPdc around the post of last skipped dc (X made), dc in next sc, FPdc around the post of next dc, ch 1, sk next ch-1 sp, dc in last st, turn.

Row 4: Rep Row 2.

Row 5: Ch 1, sc in blps of 1st 6 sc, ch 1, sk next ch-1 sp, FPdc around the post of next FPdc 2 rows below, dc in next sc in current row, FPdc around the post of each of next 2 FPdc 2 rows below, dc in next sc in current row, FPdc around the post of next FPdc 2 rows below, ch 1, sk next ch-1 sp, dc in last st, turn.

Rows 6–33: Rep Rows 2–5 (7 times) or for desired length to match circumference of the upper leg. Do not Fasten off.

FINISHED SIZE

› Instructions given fit ladies' small

› Fit should have 1"–2" (2.5cm–5cm) of negative ease. Measure the upper calf, or wherever the cuff will go, and subtract 1"–2" (2.5cm–5cm). Stitch to the circumference minus 1" or 2" (2.5cm or 5cm). If the cuff will be worn over the top of a boot, measure the boot circumference instead of the leg.

› 6½" (16.5cm) tall for 15 sts; 33 rows = 15" (38.1cm) in circumference

MATERIALS

› Rowan Big Wool (3.5 oz/87 yds/80m/ 100g per ball): 2 balls #56 Glum (A), 1 ball #25 Wild Berry (B)

› Sizes M/13 (9mm) crochet hook or size needed to obtain gauge

› Yarn needle

GAUGE

› 15 sts = 6½" (16.5cm); 33 rows = 15" (38.1cm)

› Take time to check gauge

Edging

Working across dc edge, ch 1, sc in each row-end st across. Fasten off leaving an 18" (45.7cm) sewing length. With WS together, and using sewing length and yarn needle, match sts and whipstitch last row to foundation ch. Fasten off. Turn RS out.

Trim Round: With RS facing, join B in either ch-1 sp in Row 1, working vertically in each row, surface sl st in each corresponding ch-1 sp of each row around cuff. Fasten off. Rep Trim Round around cuff in other ch-1 sps.

Finishing

Weave in ends.

BOOT CUFF STITCH DIAGRAM

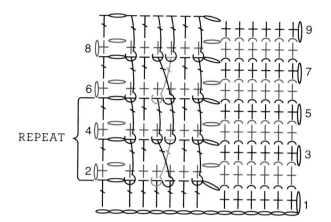

REPEAT

HOW TO CABLE

1. Double crochet.

2. Skip the next front post double crochet and work a front post double crochet around the next one.

3. Next, go back and front post double crochet around the front post double crochet that was skipped (X made).

4. Double crochet.

HOW TO SURFACE SLIP STITCH

1. Make a slip knot and place it on the Wrong Side of the project. Reach the hook from the Right Side to the back, put the knot on the hook and pull it to the front.

2. Hold the slip knot taut with one hand and tension the working yarn with the other.

3. Yarn over.

4. Pull the yarn through from the Wrong Side of the fabric to the Right Side and through the loop on the hook.

5. Reach the hook through the fabric to grab the yarn to make the next slip stitch.

DESIGNER TIP

Try it on as you go! If it's too small, add more rows. The same pattern can be made in a smaller yarn, but it will take longer and the gauge will be smaller.

Patuqun Ear Warmer

Total coverage, total style, totally done in one day. It's the keep-your-ears-warm kind of headband. A little Internet research tells me *patuqun* is one of the Eskimo language's words for "frosty sparkling snow." However you want to name it, the spike stitches resemble frost and create interest in this easy project.

PATTERN NOTES

Drop the color not being used, do not work over it. Pick it up when needed in subsequent rows.

Special Stitches

Spike cluster (Sp-cl): Insert hook and draw up a lp in each of next 5 sts as follows: 2 sts to right of next st and 1 row down; 1 st to right and 2 rows down; directly below current st and 3 rows down; 1 st to left and 2 rows down; 2 sts to left and 1 row down, (6 lps on hook); insert hook into top of next st in current row, yo, draw through st, yo, draw through all 6 lps on hook. (See stitch diagram and photos on the following pages.)

To "Pick up": Do not yo, insert hook into top of st, through the fabric, draw up a lp to level of current row, yo, draw through st.

The Sp-cl will partially cover the sts you need to work into, so you'll have to push the cl aside to find sts and keep the st count consistent.

HEADBAND

With A, ch 13.

Row 1 (WS): Sc in 2nd ch from hook and in each ch across, turn (12 sc).

Row 2: Ch 1, sc in each st across, turn.

Row 3: Ch 1, sc in each st across, changing to B in last st, turn.

Row 4: With B, ch 1, sc in each of 1st 4 sts, Sp-cl over next st, sc in each of last 7 sts, turn.

Rows 5–6: Ch 1, sc in each st across, turn.

Row 7: Ch 1, sc in each st across, changing to A in last st, turn.

Row 8: With A, ch 1, sc in each of 1st 8 sts, Sp-cl over next st, sc each of last 3 sts, turn.

Rows 9–10: Ch 1, sc in each st across, turn.

Row 11: Ch 1, sc in each st across, changing to B in last st, turn.

FINISHED SIZE

› To fit head size 21" (53.3cm)

› Headband measures 18" (45.7cm) in circumference (3" [7.6cm] negative ease)

MATERIALS

› Premier Primo Yarns (3.5 oz/273 yds/ 250m/100g per skein): 1 skein each #0008 Baby Blue (A) and #0001 White (B)

› Size H/8 (5mm) crochet hook or size needed to obtain gauge

› Yarn needle

GAUGE

› 12 sts = 4" (10.2cm); 16 rows in pattern = 4" (10.2cm) unstretched

› Take time to check gauge

Rows 12–75: Rep Rows 4–11 (8 times).

Rows 76–80: Rep Rows 4–8 once. Fasten off, leaving a sewing length. Or work until piece measures desired length or 4" (10.2cm) short of desired head circumference. Model is worked for 80 rows, to approximately 18" (45.7cm).

Assembly

With yarn needle and sewing length, without twisting headband, matching sts, whipstitch last row to foundation ch, forming a tube.

Edging

Round 1: With RS facing, join A with sc in side of any row on edge of Headband, working over floats, sc in each row-end st around; join with sl st in 1st sc (80 sc).

Round 2: (Ch 1, sl st) in each st around; join with sl st in 1st sl st. Fasten off.
Rep Edging around other side edge of Headband.

Finishing

Weave in ends.

EARWARMER STITCH DIAGRAM

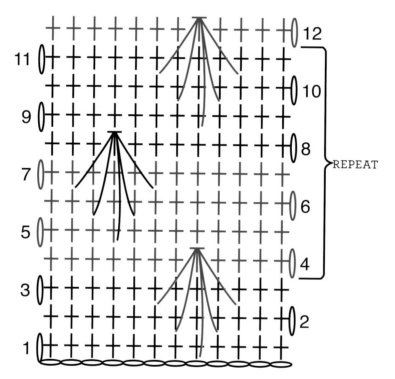

HOW TO MAKE A SPIKE STITCH

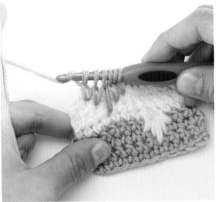

1. Use the stitch diagram for help. Insert the hook in the closest spot, yarn over and pull up a loop, yarn over and pull through first two loops on the hook.

2. Repeat the process until there are six loops on the hook, yarn over and pull through all the loops on the hook.

Fluffy Wristlet

When a project only takes one day to make, it's not a major commitment. Wear it now while the trend is hot, and it will be ready for you when the trend comes around again. Build your crochet skills with this novelty netting yarn.

PATTERN NOTES
> › All rounds are worked on the Right Side.
> › Place a marker in the first stitch of each round and move the marker up as the work progresses.
> › To work with yarn B: Place the hook through a net hole, place the hook in the unused loop of the Bag, pull the next hole strand through the unused loop and the net loop that is on the hook (sl st made).

Special Stitches
Adjustable ring: Wrap thread in ring around index finger, ending thread tail behind working thread. Remove from finger and grip the ring and tail firmly between middle finger and thumb. Insert hook through center of ring, with working thread, yo, draw up lp, work sts of 1st round in ring. After the 1st round of sts has been completed, pull gently, but firmly, on thread tail to close ring.

Single crochet 2 together (sc2tog): [Insert hook in next st, yo, draw yarn through st] twice, yo, draw yarn through 3 lps on hook.

WRISTLET (MAKE 2)
With A, make an adjustable ring.

Round 1: Work 8 sc in ring, do not join. Pm in 1st st of round and leave in place until ruffle is added.

Round 2: Working in blps only, 2 sc in each st around (16 sc). Place a 2nd marker in the 1st st of this round and move it up as the work progresses.

Round 3: Working in blps only, *sc in next st, 2 sc in next st; rep from * around (24 sc).

Round 4: Working in blps only, *sc in each of next 2 sc, 2 sc in next st; rep from * around (32 sc).

Rounds 5–9: Working in blps only, sc in each sc around.

Round 10: Working in blps only, *sc in each of next 2 sc, sc2tog over next 2 sts; rep from * around (24 sc).

Rounds 11–13: Working in blps only, sc in each sc around.

Round 14: Working blps only, sc in each of next 12 sts, ch 2, sk next 2 sts, sc in each of next 10 sts, pm in 4th from last st of Round 14 (22 sc, ch-2 sp).

FINISHED SIZE
> › Strap is 7½" (19.1cm)
> › Bag is 7" (17.8cm) wide and 6" (15.2cm) tall (excluding handle strap)

MATERIALS
> › Willow Yarns, Burrow (3.5 oz/197 yd/180m/ 100g) 1 skein #58 Peacock (A)
> › Premier Yarns, Starbella Flash (3.5 oz/33 yds/30m/ 100g per ball): 1 skein #1614 Silver (B)
> › Size I/9 (5.5mm) crochet hook or size needed to obtain gauge
> › Stitch markers
> › 1" (2.5cm) button
> › Yarn needle

GAUGE
> › 16 sts = 6" (15.2cm); 10 rows sc = 4" (10.2cm)
> › Take time to check gauge

WRISTLET STITCH DIAGRAM

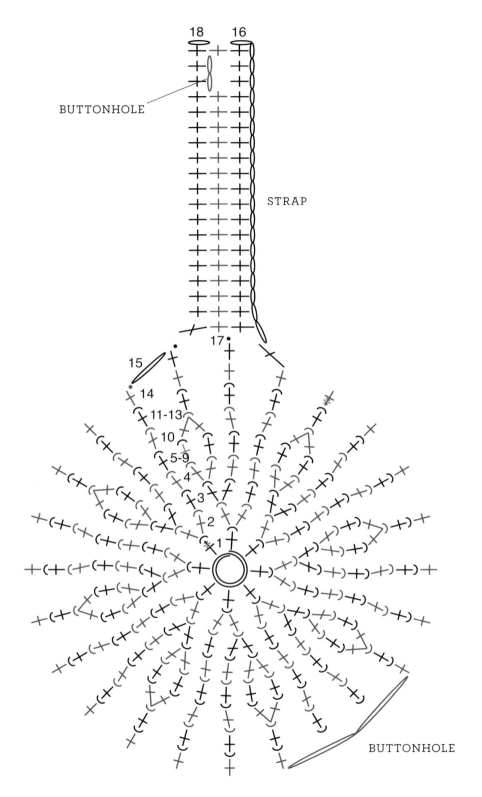

STRAP ROWS

Row 15: Ch 1, turn, working in both lps of sts, sc in each of next 3 sts, turn.

Row 16: Ch 20, sc in 2nd ch from hook, sc in each ch across to Row 15, sl st in middle sc of 3 sc in Row 15, turn.

Row 17: Sc in each of 1st 16 sts, ch 2, sk next 2 sts, sc in last st, turn.

Row 18: Ch 1, sc in 1st st, 2 sc in next ch-2 sp, sc in each of last 16 sts, sl st in last sc in Row 15. Fasten off.

RUFFLES

Working in the unused lps (flps) of Bag, join B with sl st in marked 1st st of Round 1, sl st in each unused lp around 13 spiral rounds to marked st in Round 14. Cut B, leaving a 6" (15.2cm) tail, fold the tail under to create 2 thicknesses, sl st in the 3 rem sts of Round 13, working through both thicknesses. Fasten off. Remove all markers.

Sew button on inside of bag at base of strap, opposite the button hole on bag body.

Finishing

Weave in ends. Sew button on inside of bag at base of Strap, opposite the button hole on Bag body.

HOW TO ATTACH RUFFLE YARN TO A BAG

1. Holding the net yarn against the fabric of the bag, insert the hook through the net yarn and under an unused loop on the bag.

2. Yarn over with the net yarn and pull through both the unused loop and the net yarn.

3. Insert hook into the next stitch and pull the net through both the yarn loop and the net loop that is on the hook.

Boulder Cowl

Learn to add luscious volume with popcorn stitches. Using a self-striping bulky yarn yields great results without having to change color. Bulky yarn is the trick to making fast and dramatic crochet projects. I often learn new techniques on larger yarn than the project requires. It reminds me of the days in kindergarten when the kids start with the super chunky crayons first until they get the hang of writing. It's the same with crochet; learn with bigger yarn and hooks, then scale down as you gain comfort.

PATTERN NOTES
Beginning ch-3 counts as a double crochet.

Special Stitches
Popcorn (pop): Work 5 dc in 1st st, drop lp from hook, place hook in top 2 lps of 1st dc of group, insert hook in dropped lp and draw through st.

COWL
Ch 27.

Row 1 (RS): Dc in 4th ch from hook and in each ch across, turn (25 dc).

Row 2: Ch 4 (counts as dc, ch 1), *sk next st, pop in next dc, ch 1, sk next st, dc in each of next 2 sts; rep from * across to last 4 sts, ch 1, sk next st, pop in next st, ch 1, sk next st, dc in last st, turn (5 pops; 10 dc; 10 ch-1 sps).

Row 3: Ch 3 (counts as dc), dc in each st and ch across, turn (25 dc).

Rows 4–69: Rep Rows 2 and 3.

Fasten off, leaving an 18" (45.7cm) sewing length.

Finishing
Whipstitch last row to foundation ch at base of Row 1 forming a tube. Weave in ends.

STITCH DIAGRAM

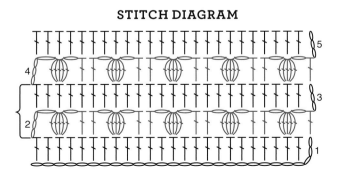

FINISHED SIZE
› 8½" × 43" (21.6cm × 109cm), before joining

MATERIALS
› Red Heart Boutique Midnight (2.5 oz/ 153 yds/140m/70g per skein): 2 skeins #1936 Misty

› Size K/10½ (6.5mm) crochet hook or size needed to obtain gauge

› Yarn needle

GAUGE
› 12 sts in pattern = 4" (10.2cm); 8 rows in pattern = 5" (12.7cm)

› Take time to check gauge

FINISHED SIZE

› 15" (38cm) in circum-
  ference at top edge

› 4¾" (12.1cm) wide at
  top edge (flat)

› 3¼" (8.3cm) wide at
  bottom edge (flat)

› 3¼" (8.3cm) deep

MATERIALS

› Berroco Weekend
  (3.5 oz/205 yds/187m/
  100g per hank): 1 hank
  #5926 Clothesline

› Size I/9 (5.5mm)
  crochet hook or size
  needed to obtain
  gauge

› Yarn needle

GAUGE

› Row 1, joined, flat
  = 3¼" (8.3cm); one
  3-tr cluster row = 1"
  (2.5cm)

› Take time to
  check gauge

Cup Cozy

A cup cozy turns any beverage into an event. With this project, you'll learn a clever way to increase in a pattern—with a filler row of basic stitches! When the stitch pattern is too cumbersome for increasing, consider adding an increase row of basic stitches before resuming the more intricate pattern.

PATTERN NOTES

All rounds are worked on the Right Side. Join rounds with slip stitches as instructed.

Special Stitches

2-dc cluster (2-dc cl): [Yo, insert hook in same sp, yo, draw yarn through sp, yo, draw through 2 lps on hook] twice in same st, yo, draw yarn through 3 lps on hook.

3-tr cluster (3-tr cl): *Yo (twice), insert hook in next st, yo, draw yarn through st, [yo, draw through 2 lps on hook] twice*; rep from * 3 times in same st, yo, draw yarn through 4 lps on hook.

Treble crochet 2 together (tr2tog): *Yo (twice), insert hook in next st, yo, draw yarn through st, yo, draw yarn through 2 lps on hook] twice; rep from * once, yo, draw yarn through 3 lps on hook.

Foundation single crochet (Fsc): Start with a slip knot, ch 2, insert hook in 2nd ch from hook, draw up a lp, yo, draw through 1 lp on hook, yo, draw through 2 lps—1 sc with its own ch at bottom. Work next st under lps of that ch. Insert hook under 2 lps at bottom of the previous st, draw up a lp, yo and draw through 1 lp, yo and draw through 2 lps.

COZY

Work 25 Fsc; without twisting, join with sl st in 1st st to form a ring.

Round 1: Ch 5 (counts as tr, ch 1), *sk next st, 3-tr cl in next st, ch 3, 3-tr cl in next st, ch 1; rep from * around, join with sl st in 4th ch of beg ch-5. Do not turn.

Round 2: Ch 3 (counts as dc), *dc in next ch-1 sp, dc in next 3-tr cl, 2-dc cl in next ch-3 sp, dc in next 3-tr cl, dc in next ch-1 sp**, dc in next tr; rep from * around, ending last rep at **; join with sl st in top of beg-dc (30 sts).

Round 3: Ch 4, tr in next st (counts as tr2tog), ch 1, *sk next st, 3-tr cl in next st, ch 3, 3-tr cl in next st, ch 1, sk 1 st, tr2tog over next 2 sts, ch 1, sk 1 st; rep from * around; join with sl st in 1st tr2tog.

Round 4: Ch 1, (sc, ch 3, sc) in 1st st, *sc in next ch-1 sp, sk next 3-tr cl, (sc, ch 3, sc) in next ch-3 sp, sk next 3-tr cl, sc in next ch-1 sp**, (sc, ch 3, sc) in next st; rep from * around, ending last rep at **; join with sl st in 1st sc. Fasten off.

Bottom Edging

Round 1: Working in underside of sc foundation, join with sc in any ch, sc in each st around; join with sl st in 1st sc. Fasten off.

Finishing

Weave in ends.

CUP COZY STITCH DIAGRAM

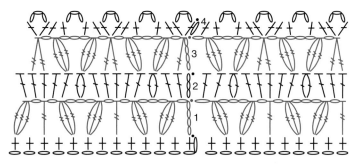

REDUCED SAMPLE OF PATTERN

SKILL LEVEL

Carolyn Necklace

In the style of a vintage collar, adorn your neck with this lovely necklace. This project is named for my Great Aunt Carolyn. She was my mother's aunt and the first woman in our family to go to college. She was known for her colorful language and her even more outlandish wardrobe. To truly do her justice, I would have had to add a dozen or so diamonds to this necklace, or at least a topaz the size of a quarter.

FINISHED SIZE
› 16" (40.6cm) long; 1¼" (3.2cm) at widest point

MATERIALS
› Universal Yarn Nazli Gelin Garden 3, 100% Mercerized Egyptian Giza Cotton (1.76 oz/ 136 yds/124m/50g per ball): 1 ball #19 Light Tan
› Size F/5 (3.75mm) crochet hook crochet hook or size needed to obtain gauge
› Lobster clasp
› Yarn needle

GAUGE
› 3 rows = 1¼" (3.2cm), 75 ch plus clasp = 16" (40.6cm)
› Take time to check gauge

PATTERN NOTES

Special Stitches

Shell (sh): ([dc, ch 1] 3 times, dc) in same st.

Picot: Ch 3, hdc in 3rd ch from hook.

NECKLACE

To begin, tie on the lobster clasp. Make a slip knot immediately next to the clasp.

Ch 79.

Row 1: Working in back ridge of ch sts, sl st in 4th ch from hook (lp made for clasp), sl st in each of next 19 ch, *sk next 2 ch, sh in next ch, sl st in each of next 2 sts; rep from * 4 times; sl st in each of last 20 ch.

Row 2: Ch 1, rotate to work across opposite side of foundation ch, sl st in each ch across, sl st in each ch of lp.

Row 3: Working across Row 1, sl st in each sl st across to 1st dc of the 1st sh, *[(sc, picot, sc) in dc, sc in next ch-1 sp] 3 times, (sc, picot, sc) in last dc of sh, sk next 2 sl sts; rep from * 4 times; sl st in each sl st across Row 1. Fasten off.

Finishing

Weave in ends.

NECKLACE STITCH DIAGRAM

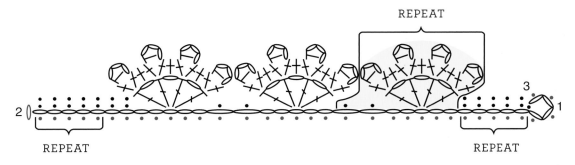

Oval Bib

Ovals are so much fun! I love ovals and try to find places to put them. An oval also makes an excellent bottom to a tote bag! Give this oval a try then embellish it with some wiggly crochet to be a "crumb catcher". You'll learn to work in an oval and add ruffles. For a boy, leave off the ruffles and change colors every row to make an eye-catching oval bulls-eye design.

FINISHED SIZE
› 7" × 9" (17.8cm × 22.9cm) excluding ties

MATERIALS
› Universal Yarn Cotton Supreme (3.5 oz/ 180 yds/165m/100g per hank): 1 hank #518 Spring Green
› Size I/9 (5.5mm) crochet hook or size needed to obtain gauge
› Locking stitch marker
› Yarn needle

GAUGE
› In Strap pattern, 16 sts = 5" (12.7cm)
› 6 rows = 3½" (8.9cm)
› Take time to check gauge

PATTERN NOTES

› All rounds are worked on the Right Side, do not turn.

› Rounds are joined with a slip stitch.

Special Stitches
Foundation double crochet (Fdc):

Step 1: Ch 3 (counts as 1st Fdc), yo, insert hook in 3rd ch from hook, yo and draw up a lp, yo and draw through 1 lp on hook (base ch made), [yo and draw through 2 lps on hook] twice (Fdc made).

Step 2: Yo, insert hook in base ch of last Fdc made (be sure to insert hook under 2 lps of the base ch; the lp at the front or face of the base ch and the lp on the bottom side of the base ch), yo and draw up a lp, yo and draw through 1 lp on hook (base ch made), [yo and draw through 2 lps on hook] twice (Fdc made).
Rep Step 2 for desired number of Fdc.

BIB STITCH DIAGRAM

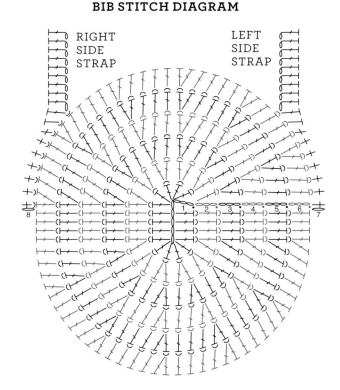

RUFFLE ENDS STITCH DIAGRAM

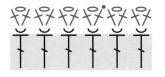

BIB
Ch 8.

Round 1: Work 5 dc in 4th ch from hook, dc in each of next 3 sts, 6 dc in last ch, working across opposite side of foundation ch, dc in each of next 5 ch; join with sl st in top beg ch-3 (18 dc).

Round 2: Ch 3 (counts as dc here and throughout), working in blps only, dc in 1st st, 2 dc in each of next 5 dc, dc in each of next 3 sts, 2 dc in each of next 6 dc, dc in each of last 3 sts; join with sl st in top of beg ch-3 (30 dc).

Round 3: Ch 3, working in blps only, 2 dc in next dc, [dc in next st, 2 dc in next st] 5 times, dc in each of next 3 sts, [dc in next st, 2 dc in next st] 6 times, dc in each of last 3 dc; join with sl st in top of beg ch-3 (42 dc).

Round 4: Ch 3, working in blps only, dc in next st, 2 dc in next st, [dc in each of next 2 sts, 2 dc in next st] 5 times, dc in each of next 3 sts, [dc in next 2 sts, 2 dc in next st] 6 times, dc in each of last 3 dc; join with sl st in top of beg ch-3 (54 dc).

Round 5: Ch 3, working in blps only, dc in each of next 2 sts, 2 dc in next st [dc in each of next 3 sts, 2 dc in next st] 5 times, dc in each of next 3 sts, [dc in each of next 3 sts, 2 dc in next st] 6 times, dc in each of last 3 dc; join with sl st in top of beg ch-3 (66 dc).

Round 6: Ch 3, working in blps only, dc in each of next 3 sts, 2 dc in next st, [dc in each of next 4 sts, 2 dc in next st] 5 times, place a marker in st number 37, dc in each of next 4 sts, [dc in each of next 4 sts, 2 dc in next st] 6 times, dc in each of last 3 dc; join with sl st in top of beg ch-3 (78 dc).

Left Side Strap
Row 7: Ch 1, working in blps only, sc in each of next 7 sts, hdc in next st, dc in next st, Fdc in base of last dc, work 33 Fdc. Fasten off.

Right Side Strap
Row 8: With WS facing, join yarn with sl st in flps only of marked 37th st of Round 6, ch 1, working in flps only of sts, sc in each of 1st 7 sts, hdc in next st, dc in next st, Fdc in base of last dc, work 33 Fdc. If ruffles are not desired, fasten off.

RUFFLES
Round 1: Beg with the inner most unused lps of Round 1, join yarn with sc in any st, ch 1, sc in same st, (sc, ch 1, sc) in each st around; join with sl st in 1st sc. Fasten off.
Rep Round 1 for each subsequent round of unused lps. Rep Round 1 in flps only of sts in Round 6.
Weave in ends.

Yesterday Bruges Scarf

Take the road less traveled with this fun Bruges Lace scarf. You won't need any new tools or fancy stitches to learn this intriguing style of crochet. Use a multicolor yarn to help you see the basic double crochet stitches as they are formed. This technique is so much fun. You'll be researching more Bruges Lace patterns in no time.

PATTERN NOTES
The ch-5 side loops are worked at the beginning of a row.

Helpful Hints:
› Curve changes direction after eight rows, then after every eleven rows.
› The first join of each repeat is done using a slip stitch, and the second using a treble crochet.
› There will be two unused loops on the outside of the curve for each rep.

SCARF
Ch 5.

Row 1 (RS): Sc in 2nd ch from hook, hdc in next ch, dc in each of the last 2 ch, turn.

Row 2: Ch 5, dc in each of 1st 2 sts, hdc in next st, sc in last st, turn.

Row 3: Ch 1, sc in 1st st, hdc in next st, dc in each of last 2 sts, turn.

Rows 4–7: Rep Rows 2–3 (twice).

Row 8: Rep Row 2. Change curve direction:

Rows 9–18: Rep Rows 2–3 (5 times).

Row 19: Rep Row 2. Change curve direction and begin connecting edge lps as follows:

Row 20: Ch 2, sl st in next 1st ch-5 lp on adjacent edge, ch 2, turn, dc in each of the 1st 2 sts, hdc in next st, sc in last st.

Row 21: Rep Row 3.

Row 22: Ch 2, tr in next unjoined ch-5 lp on adjacent edge, ch 2, turn, dc in each of the 1st 2 sts, hdc in next st, sc in last st.

Row 23: Rep Row 3.

Rows 24–29: Rep Rows 2–3 (3 times).

Row 30: Rep Row 2.

Rows 31–206: Rep Rows 20–30 (16 times) (or to desired length).

SKILL LEVEL

FINISHED SIZE
› 4½" × 51" (11.4cm × 129.5cm)

MATERIALS
› Red Heart Boutique Unforgettable (3.5 oz/ 279 yds/256m/100g per ball): 1 ball of #3950 Petunia
› Size I/9 (5.5mm) crochet hook or size needed to obtain gauge
› Yarn needle

GAUGE
› 4 sts = 1" (2.5cm); 6 rows dc = 4" (10.2cm)
› Take time to check gauge

Beginning Circle

Ch 5.

Rows 1–8: Rep Rows 1–8 of scarf.

Row 9: Rep Row 3.

Rows 10–11: Rep Rows 2–3.

Row 12: Ch 2, sl st in ch-5 lp at edge of Scarf Row 11, ch 2, turn, dc in each of 1st 2 sts, hdc in next st, sc in last st.

Row 13: Rep Row 3.

Row 14: Ch 2, sl st in ch-5 lp at edge of Scarf Row 9, ch 2, turn, dc in each of 1st 2 sts, hdc in next st, sc in last st.

Row 15: Rep Row 3.

Row 16: Ch 2, sl st in sc of Row 1 of Scarf, ch 2, turn, dc in each of the 1st 2 sts, hdc in next st, sc in last st. Fasten off, leaving a sewing length. With sewing length and yarn needle, whipstitch last row of circle to foundation ch at base of Row 1. Tack unjoined corner of 1st scarf row to edge of circle.

Ending Circle

Make same as Beginning Circle, joining to last st of last row and last 2 ch-5 lps at end of Scarf.

Finishing

Weave in ends.

HOW TO JOIN IN BRUGES LACE

1. At the end of a curve, chain two to make half of a side loop.

2. Insert the hook into a previously made chain-five side loop.

3. Pull through the side loop and the loop on the hook to create the slip stitch; join.

4. Chain two to make the second half of the side loop and turn the work.

5. Work the next row and resume pattern.

SCARF STITCH DIAGRAM

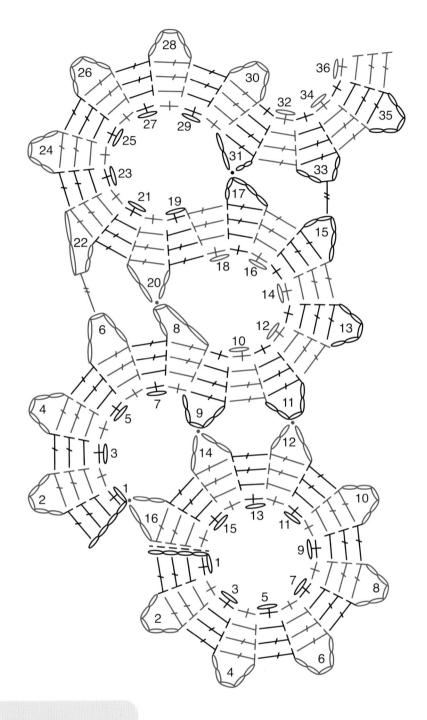

DESIGNER TIP

If needed, place a marker in the ch-5 side loops of key rows so you can find it easily.

Jessica Tunisian Mitts

Get out your afghan crochet hook to make these stretchy ribbed Tunisian mitts. Work the fabric flat and seam it up! In just one day, you'll master these beginner Tunisian stitches and have proof at your fingertips.

FINISHED SIZE
› Instructions given fit ladies' size small; 7½" (19.1cm) in circumference around hand

MATERIALS
› Lorna's Laces Shepherd Sport 100% Superwash Merino Wool (2 oz/200 yds/ 183m/57g): 1 hank of Turquoise
› Sizes H/8 (5mm) flexible or straight Tunisian crochet hook, 12"–14" (30.5cm–35.6cm) in length or size needed to obtain gauge
› Yarn needle

GAUGE
› 19 sts and 14 rows in pattern = 4" (10.2cm)
› Take time to check gauge

PATTERN NOTES

› Pattern is a multiple of 4 plus 1 stitches.

› Skip first vertical bar of each row.

› The first loop on the hook beginning a row counts as the first stitch.

Special Stitches

Note: Each Tunisian Row is worked in two parts—the Forward (Fwd) pass and the Return (Ret) pass.

Tunisian simple stitch (Tss): Fwd: *Insert hook under next vertical bar, yo, draw yarn though st; rep from * across to last st, insert hook in 2 lps of last st, yo, draw yarn through st.

Basic Ret: Yo, draw yarn through 1 lp on hook, *yo, draw yarn through 2 lps on hook, rep from * across (1 lp remains on hook and counts as 1st st of next row).

Tunisian knit stitch (Tks): Fwd: Insert hook from front to back between 2 vertical bars, yo, draw yarn through st. Ret: Work Basic Ret.

Tunisian purl stitch (Tps): Fwd: Bring yarn to front, insert hook under next vertical bar, yo, draw yarn though st; Ret: Work Basic Ret.

Tunisian Purl two together (Tps2tog): Fwd: Bring yarn to front, insert hook under 2 vertical bars, yo, draw yarn through sts. Ret: Work Basic Ret.

MITTS (MAKE 2)

Ch 36.

Row 1 (RS): Fwd: Starting in 2nd ch from hook, pick up a lp in each ch across, do not turn (35 lps on hook). Ret: Work Basic Ret on all rows unless otherwise stated. Row 1 of stitch diagram complete.

Rows 2–13: Fwd: Sk 1st vertical bar (1st lp on hook counts as 1st Tss) [Tps in next 2 sts, Tks in next 2 sts] rep across to last 3 sts, Tps in next 2 sts, Tss in last st. Ret: Work Basic Ret.

Rows 14–17: Fwd: Tps2tog in next 2 sts, resume pattern to last 3 sts, Tps2tog, Tss in last st. Ret: Work Basic Ret.

Rows 18–21: Work even following stitch diagram.

Row 22: Fwd: *Tps in next 2 sts, Tks in next 2 sts; rep from * across to last 3 sts, Tps in next 2 sts, Tss in last st. Ret: *Yo, pull through 5 lps, ch 3; 5 times, yo, pull through 4 lps.

Row 23 (standard crochet row): Ch 1, sc in 1st ch-3 sp, [5 dc in next ch-3 sp, sc in next ch-3 sp] twice, 5 dc in next ch-3 sp, sc in last st. Fasten off, leaving a 15" (38.1) sewing length.

Finishing

With sewing length and yarn needle, with WS facing, matching rows, whipstitch Rows 1–5, skip Rows 6–12, whipstitch Rows 13–23. Fasten off. Turn RS out. Weave in ends.

DESIGNER TIP

After a few rows, measure the piece around the fullest part of the hand for proper fit. For larger mitts, increase in increments of 4 sts (approximately 1" [2.5cm]).

HOW TO MAKE TUNISIAN KNIT AND PURL STITCHES

1. Yarn over and pull through one loop on the hook, leaving the remaining loops on the hook.

2. For the Tunisian purl stitch, the working yarn comes to the front of the fabric, then insert the hook into the vertical bar.

3. To finish the Tunisian purl stitch, grab the yarn and pull it through the vertical bar.

4. Again, for Tunisian purl stitch, the working yarn comes to the front; insert the hook in the vertical bar.

5. It may help to anchor the working yarn at the front with your thumb as you yarn over and pull through.

6. The gold hook indicates where to insert the hook for the Tunisian knit stitch, all the way through the fabric to the back.

7. With the yarn in its usual place, (not in front) insert the hook from the front of the fabric to the back underneath the next vertical bar as shown in step 6.

8. Yarn over and pull up a loop through to the front of the fabric.

9. When working the Forward pass, each stitch leaves one loop on the hook until it's time to work them off in the Return pass. One loop = one stitch.

MITTS STITCH DIAGRAM

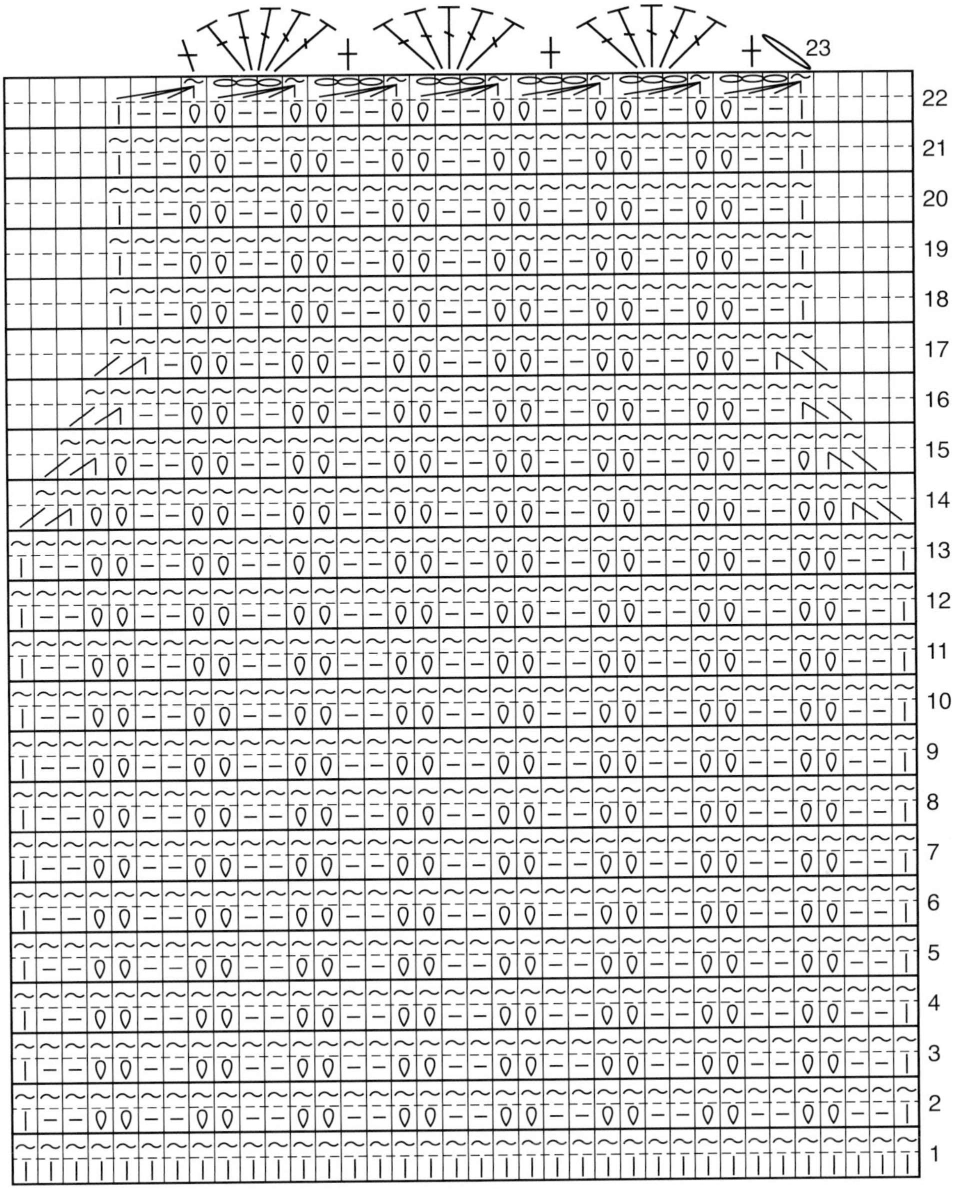

DIAGRAM KEY

0 = LOOP ON HOOK AT BEG OF ROUND

$\widetilde{1}$ = TSS

$\widetilde{0}$ = TKS

Falling Stars Keyhole Scarf

Cascading stars create an easy keyhole scarf in a luxurious yarn for a fantastic quick gift. Practice working with two strands held together to add speed to a project and create a squishy texture. Join-as-you-go motifs make quick work of this cuddly creation.

FINISHED SIZE
› 8½" × 31" (21.6cm × 78.7cm), blocked

MATERIALS
› Bijou Spun Lhasa Wilderness (2 oz/ 180 yds/165m/56g per ball): 1 hank #12 Sky

› Size I/9 (5.5mm) crochet hook or size needed to obtain gauge

› Yarn needle

GAUGE
› First two rounds of Medium Star = 3½" (8.9cm) in diameter

› Small Star = 6¼" (15.9cm) point to point

› Medium Star = 8" (20.3cm) point to point

› Large Star = 9" (22.9cm) point to point

› Take time to check gauge

PATTERN NOTES
› Project is worked with two strands held together.
› All rounds worked on the Right Side.

Special Stitches
Picot: Ch 3, hdc in 3rd ch from hook.

Cluster (cl): *Yo (twice), insert hook in same sp, yo, draw up a lp, [yo, draw through 2 lps on hook] 3 times; rep from * once, yo, draw through 4 lps on hook.

SMALLEST STAR (MAKE 1)
With 2 strands of yarn, ch 5; join with sl st in 1st ch to form a ring.

Round 1: Ch 3 (counts as 1st dc), 11 dc in ring; join with sl st in top of beg ch-3 (12 dc).

Round 2: Ch 1, sc in 1st st, ch 7, sk next st; *sc in next st, ch 7, sk next st; rep from * around; join with sl st in 1st sc (6 sc, 6 ch-7 sps).

Round 3: Ch 1, sc in 1st sc, *(4 dc, picot, 4 dc) in next ch-7 sp, sc in next sc; rep from * around; join with sl st in 1st sc (48 dc, 6 picot, 6 sc).

FIRST MEDIUM STAR (MAKE 2)
With 2 strands of yarn, ch 5; join with sl st in 1st ch to form a ring.

Round 1: Ch 3, 11 dc in ring; join with sl st in top of beg ch-3 (12 dc).

Round 2: Ch 6 (counts as dc, ch 3), cl in next st, *ch 3, dc in next st, ch 3, cl in next st; rep from * around, ch 3; join with sl st in 3rd ch of beg ch-6 (6 dc, 6 cl, 12 ch-3 sps).

Round 3: Sl st in next ch-3 sp, ch 3, 2 dc in same sp, dc in next cl, 3 dc in next ch-3 sp, ch 5, *3 dc in next ch-3 sp, dc in next cl, 3 dc in next ch-3 sp, ch 5; rep from * around, 3 dc in same sp, dc in next cl, 3 dc in next ch-3 sp, ch 5; join with sl st in top of beg ch-3 (42 dc; 6 ch-5 sps).

Round 4 (joining round): Sl st in each of next 3 sts, ch 1, sc in same st, ch 3, *(4 dc, ch 1, sl st in any picot of Small Star, ch 1, 4 dc) in ch-5 sp, ch 3, sk next 3 dc, sc in next dc; rep from * once, joining to next picot on Small Star, **ch 3, (4 dc, ch 3, 4 dc) in next ch-5 sp, ch 3, sk next 3 dc***, sc in next dc; rep from ** around, ending last rep at *** (4 dc, ch 3, 4 dc) in ch-5 sp, ch 3; join with sl st in 1st sc. Fasten off.

SECOND MEDIUM STAR (MAKE 1)

Work same as First Medium Star, joining to 2 ch-3 spaces of last Medium Star opposite Small Star.

LARGE STAR (MAKE 1)

With 2 strands of yarn, ch 25; join with sl st in 1st ch to form a ring.

Round 1: Ch 3, 35 dc in ring; join with sl st in top of beg ch-3 (36 dc).

Round 2: Ch 6 (counts as dc, ch 3), sk next st, *cl in next st, sk next st, cl in next st, ch 3, sk next st**, dc in next st, ch 3, sk 1 st; rep from * around, ending last rep at **, cl in next st, sk next st, cl in next st, ch 3; join with sl st in 3rd ch of beg ch-6 (12 cl; 6 dc; 12 ch-3 sps).

Round 3: Sl st in next ch-3 sp, ch 3, 2 dc in same sp, *sc in each of next 2 cl, 3 dc in next ch-3 sp, ch 5**, 3 dc in next ch-3 sp; rep from * around, ending last rep at **; join with sl st in top of beg ch-3 (36 dc; 12 sc; 6 ch-5 sps).

Join Large Star to 2 ch-3 spaces of last Medium Star opposite junction to previous Star as follows:

Round 4 (joining round): Sl st in each of next 3 sts, ch 1, sc in 1st 2 sc, *ch 3, sk next 3 dc, (4 dc, ch 1, sl st in ch-3 sp of Medium Star, ch 1, 4 dc), ch 3, sk next 3 sts, sc in each of next 2 sts; rep from * once, **ch 3, sk next 3 dc, (4 dc, ch 3, 4 dc) in next ch-5 sp, ch 3, sk next 3 sts***, sc in each of next 2 sts; rep from ** around, ending last rep at ***; join with sl st in 1st sc.

Finishing

Weave in ends. Block.

DESIGNER TIP

Instead of using two strands of dk weight yarn, use one strand of worsted weight yarn to result in a similar-sized finished project.

**SMALL AND MEDIUM STAR
STITCH DIAGRAM**

JOINING OF SECOND
MEDIUM STAR

4

LARGE STAR STITCH DIAGRAM

FIRST
MEDIUM
STAR

1
2
3   4

3
2
1

2
3   4

SMALL
STAR

LARGE STAR

SECOND MEDIUM STAR

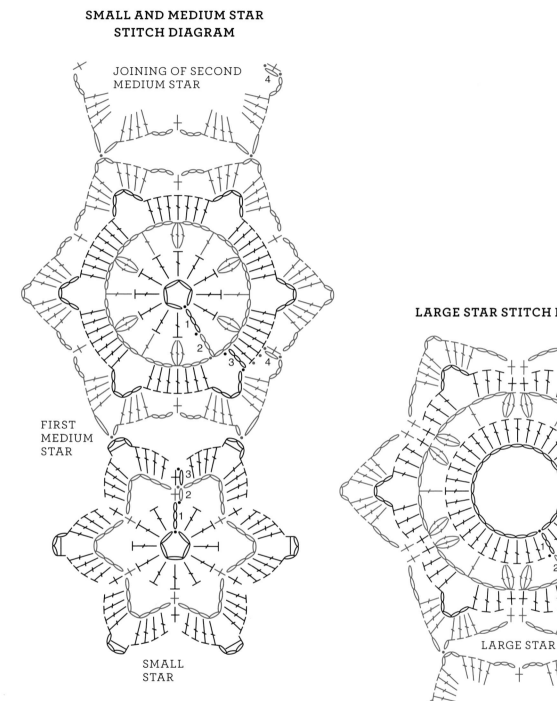

Hold on to Your Hat

Take your Tunisian crochet skills to the next level with this Tunisian in-the-round hat. While there are many methods to Tunisian in the round, this one will get you started and create a stretchy, dense, warm fabric in the process.

PATTERN NOTES

› If you are new to Tunisian crochet, a multicolored yarn will be more forgiving than a solid color.

› All rounds are worked on Right Side without turning.

› Tunisian rounds are worked in two parts: A Forward (Fwd) pass and a Return (Ret) pass.

› Join with Tunisian join unless otherwise indicated.

Special Stitches & Techniques

Adjustable ring: Wrap thread in ring around index finger, ending thread tail behind working thread. Remove from finger and grip the ring and tail firmly between middle finger and thumb. Insert hook through center of ring; with working thread, yo, draw up lp, work sts of 1st round in ring. After the 1st round of sts has been completed, pull gently but firmly on thread tail to close ring.

Single crochet 2 together (sc2tog): [Insert hook in next st, yo, draw yarn through st] twice, yo, draw yarn through 3 lps on hook.

Tunisian Crochet

Tunisian simple stitch (Tss): Fwd: Insert hook under next vertical bar, yo, draw yarn though st. For the final st, insert hook in 2 lps of last st, yo, draw yarn through st.

Basic Ret: Ch 1 *yo, draw yarn through 2 lps on hook, rep from * across (1 lp remains on hook and counts as 1st st of next row).

Tunisian knit stitch (Tks): Fwd: Insert hook from front to back between 2 vertical bars, yo, draw yarn through st. Ret: Work Basic Ret.

Tunisian knit increase (Tki): Insert hook in sp between 2 vertical bars, yo, draw through st. Ret: Work Basic Ret.

X stitch (X-st): Insert hook under next 2 vertical bars at the same time, yo, draw up a lp, insert hook again under the 1st of the 2 bars, yo, draw up a lp (X-st made). Ret: Work Basic Ret.

Tunisian Join: On the Fwd pass, when working Tss in final bar, also insert the hook in the back side of 1st lp at beg of round, yo, draw yarn through.

FINISHED SIZE

› Newborn (baby, child, young adult) 14" (16", 18", 20") (35.6cm [40.6cm, 45.7cm, 51cm]) head circumference

› 5½" (6¼", 7¼", 8¼") (14cm [16cm, 18.4cm, 21cm]) length, crown to brim

MATERIALS

› Universal Yarn Deluxe Worsted (3.5 oz/220 yds/201m/100g per hank): 1 hank each #12270 Natural (A) and #12235 Sidewalk Gray (B) or Red Heart Boutique Unforgettable (3.5 oz/279 yds/256m/100g per skein): 1 skein #3955 Winery (for both A and B)

› Size J/10 (6mm) crochet hook and 20" (50.8cm) flexible cable Tunisian hook if using Deluxe Worsted, or size needed to obtain gauge

› Size K/10½ (6.5mm) crochet hook and 20" (50.8cm) flexible cable Tunisian hook if using Unforgettable, or size needed to obtain gauge

› Yarn needle

GAUGE

› First 10 rounds = 5" (12.7cm) in diameter

› 16 Tks = 4" (10.2cm)

› Take time to check gauge.

HAT

With standard hook (of appropriate size for yarn used) and A, make an adjustable ring.

Round 1 (RS): Ch 1, 8 sc in ring; join with sl st in 1st sc (8 sc).

Round 2: Ch 1, 2 sc in each sc around; join with sl st in 1st sc (16 sc).

Round 3: Ch 1, sc in 1st sc, 2 sc in next sc, * sc in next sc, 2 sc in next sc; rep from * around; join with sl st in 1st sc (24 sc).

Change to Tunisian hook (of appropriate size for yarn used).

Round 4: Fwd: Sk 1st st, draw up a lp in each sc to last sc, draw up a lp and join in last sc (24 lps on hook). Ret: Work Basic Ret.

Round 5: Fwd: Sk 1st st, Tks in next st, Tki, Tks in next st; [Tks in next 2 sts, Tki, Tks in next st] 7 times, joining in last st (32 lps). Ret: Work Basic Ret. Note: Sts are indicated as Tss on diagram.

Round 6: Fwd: Sk 1st st, Tks in each st around; draw up a lp and join in last sc (32 lps). Ret: Work Basic Ret.

Round 7: Fwd: Sk 1st st, Tks in each of next 2 sts, Tki, Tks in next st, *Tks in each of next 3 sts, Tki, Tks in next st; rep from * around; draw up a lp and join in last sc (40 lps). Ret: Work Basic Ret.

Round 8: Rep Round 6.

Round 9: Fwd: Sk 1st st, Tks in each of next 2 sts, Tki, Tks in next st, *Tks in each of next 3 sts, Tki, Tks in next st; rep from * around; draw up a lp and join in last sc (48 lps). Ret: Work Basic Ret.

Round 10: Fwd: Sk 1st st, Tks in each of next 2 sts, Tki, Tks in next st, *Tks in each of next 3 sts, Tki, Tks in next st; rep from * around; draw up a lp and join in last st (56 lps). Ret: Work Basic Ret.

For 3 largest sizes only:

Round 11: Rep Round 6.

Round 12: Fwd: Sk 1st st, Tks in each of next 2 sts, Tki, Tks in next st, *Tks in each of next 3 sts, Tki, Tks in next st; rep from * around; draw up a lp and join in last st (64 lps). Ret: Work Basic Ret.

For 2 largest sizes only:

Round 13: Rep Round 6.

Round 14: Fwd: Sk 1st st, Tks in each of next 2 sts, Tki, Tks in next st, *Tks in each of next 3 sts, Tki, Tks in next st; rep from * around; draw up a lp and join in last st (72 lps). Ret: Work Basic Ret.

For largest size only:

Round 15: Rep Round 6.

Round 16: Fwd: Sk 1st st, Tks in each of next 2 sts, Tki, Tks in next st, *Tks in each of next 3 sts, Tki, Tks in next st; rep from * around; draw up a lp and join in last st (84 lps). Ret: Work Basic Ret.

For all sizes:

Rounds 11–17 (13–21, 15–25, 17–29): Rep Round 6. Fasten off A.

Round 18 (22, 26, 30): With RS facing, join B with sl st in 1st st, rep Round 6.

BRIM

Round 1: Fwd: *X-st in next 2 sts; rep from * around to last st; draw up a lp and join in last st. Ret: Work Basic Ret.

Round 2: Fwd: Sk 1st st, Tss in next st, *X-st in next 2 sts; rep from * around to last 2 sts, Tss in next st; draw up a lp and join in last st. Ret: Work Basic Ret.

Rounds 3–6: Rep Rounds 1–2 (twice).

For smaller hat only:

Final Round: Sk 1st st, *sc2tog over next 2 sts; rep from * to last st, sc in last st; join with sl st in 1st sc (28 [32, 36, 40] sts).

For larger hat only:

Final Round: Sk 1st st, sc in each st around, join with sl st in 1st sc (55 [63, 71, 79] sts). Fasten off.

Finishing

Weave in ends.

HAT STITCH DIAGRAM

WHITE HAT—FINAL ROUND

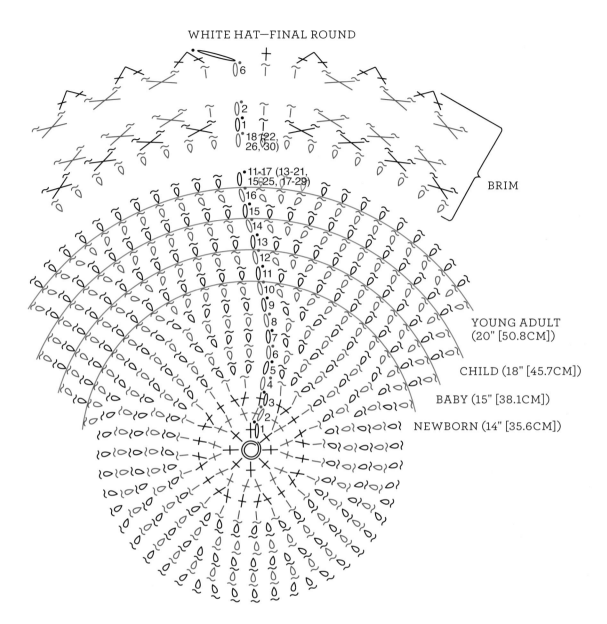

BRIM

YOUNG ADULT
(20" [50.8CM])

CHILD (18" [45.7CM])

BABY (15" [38.1CM])

NEWBORN (14" [35.6CM])

DIAGRAM KEY

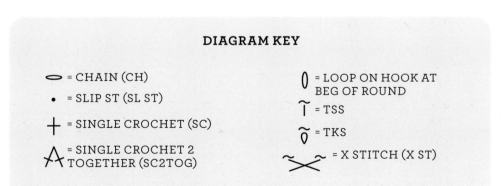

⬭ = CHAIN (CH)

• = SLIP ST (SL ST)

+ = SINGLE CROCHET (SC)

⋀ = SINGLE CROCHET 2
TOGETHER (SC2TOG)

0̸ = LOOP ON HOOK AT
BEG OF ROUND

~I = TSS

~0 = TKS

✕ = X STITCH (X ST)

HOW TO TUNISIAN CROCHET IN THE ROUND

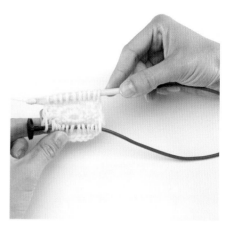

1. After three rounds of standard crochet in a circle, you may have a stitch marker in the first stitch of the previous round. Insert the hook in the next stitch and pull up a loop.

2. Pull up a loop (and leave it on the hook) in each stitch around.

3. About halfway around the circle, pull the cable through the loops as long as you can so that you have a big gap of cable that will help you make the turn and pull up loops on the other half of the circle.

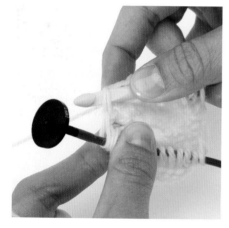

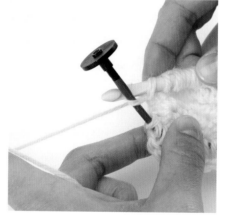

4. As you are pulling up a loop in the last stitch of the circle, insert the hook into the last stitch.

5. Insert the hook in the first loop you made, joining them together.

6. This shows a close-up of the join.

 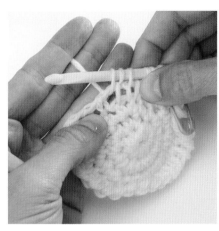 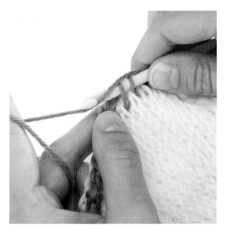

7. For a Tunisian knit stitch, insert the hook through to the back of the fabric under the vertical bar.

8. To increase, pull up a loop in the space between vertical bars. If it helps, place a marker in every increase of the round so they are easier to find on subsequent rounds.

9. To create the X, insert the hook under the next two vertical bars at the same time.

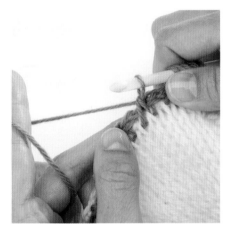 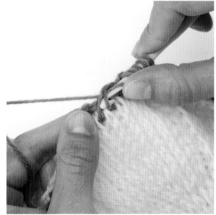 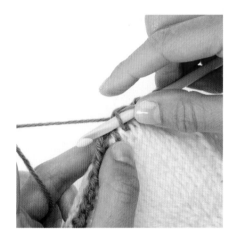

10. Yarn over and pull a loop through the two vertical bars and leave it on the hook.

11. Insert the hook under just the first vertical bar of the two that were just used.

12. Yarn over.

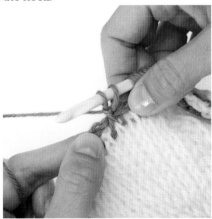

13. Pull the yarn through one vertical bar. The X is now made.

BRIM STITCH DIAGRAM

Shrug it Off

A mix of broomstick lace and traditional crochet will get this shrug done in a day! If a shrug isn't your cup of tea, learn the process, practice the pattern and make a scarf or rectangular stole.

FINISHED SIZE:
› 28" (71.1cm) wide, with edgings
› Depth: 11½" (29.2cm)

MATERIALS
› Baah Sonoma (3.5 oz/ 234 yds/213m/100g per hank): 2 hanks #3730 Singin' the Blues
› Size J/10 (6mm) crochet hook and size US 17 (12.75mm) knitting needle
› Yarn needle

GAUGE
› 15 sts and 8 rows in pattern = 4" (10.2cm)
› Take time to check gauge

PATTERN NOTES

Turn only when instructed.

Special Stitches
Broomstick Lace:

Row 1 (lp row) (RS): With crochet hook in right hand and knitting needle in left hand, draw up lp on hook and place it on knitting needle, sk 1st sc of sc row, *insert hook in next sc to right, yo, draw up a long lp and place on needle; rep from * across.

Row 2 (RS): Insert hook in 1st 4 lps on needle and slide off needle (4 lps on hook), yo with working yarn and draw through 4 lps on hook, ch 1, 4 sc in same sp, *insert hook into next 4 lps and slide off of needle, work 4 sc in same sp; rep from * across, turn.

SHRUG

Back
With J hook, ch 101.

Set-up Row: Sc in 2nd ch from hook and in each ch across, do not turn (100 sc).

Note: If desired, a foundation sc row of 100 sts may be used for Set-up Row.

Row 1 (lp row) (RS): With J hook in right hand and knitting needle in left hand, draw lp up on hook and place it on knitting needle, sk 1st sc of sc row, *insert hook in next sc to right, yo, draw up a long lp and place on needle; rep from * across (100 lps on needle).

Row 2 (RS): Insert hook in 1st 4 lps on needle and slide off needle (4 lps on hook), yo with working yarn and draw through 4 lps on hook, ch 1, 4 sc in same sp, *insert hook into next 4 lps and slide off of needle, work 4 sc in same sp; rep from * across, turn (100 sc).

Row 3: Ch 5 (counts as dc, ch 2), sk 1st 3 sts, *dc in each of next 2 sts, ch 2, sk next 2 sts; rep from * across to last st, dc in last st, turn (25 ch-2 sps).

Row 4: Ch 3 (counts as dc), dc in each st and each ch across, ending with dc in 3rd ch of turning ch, do not turn (100 dc). Rep Rows 1–4 for pattern.

Rows 5–22: Rep Rows 1–4 (4 times); then rep Rows 1–2 (once).

Divide for Fronts.

Left Front
Row 23: Ch 5, sk 1st 3 sts, *dc in each of next 2 sts, ch 2, sk next 2 sts; rep from * 6 times, dc in next st, turn, leaving rem sts unworked (8 ch-2 sps).

Row 24: Ch 3, dc in each st and each ch across, ending with dc in 3rd ch of turning ch, do not turn (32 dc).

Rows 25–27: Rep Rows 1–3 of pattern (32 sts).

Row 28 (dec row): Ch 3, [dc2tog in next ch-2 sp, dc2tog over next 2 dc] twice, dc in each st and each ch across, do not turn (28 dc).

Rows 29–32: Rep Rows 25–29 (twice) (20 sts). Fasten off, leaving an 18" (45.7cm) sewing length.

Right Front
Row 23: With WS facing, sk 36 sts to the left of last st in Left Front, join yarn with sl st in next sc, ch 5, sk 1st 3 sts, *dc in each of next 2 sts, ch 2, sk next 2 sts; rep from * across to last st, dc in last st, turn (8 ch-2 sps).

Row 24: Ch 3, dc in each st and each ch across, ending with dc in 3rd ch of turning ch, do not turn (32 dc).

Rows 25–27: Rep Rows 1–3 of pattern (32 sts).

Row 28 (dec row): Ch 3, dc in each st and each ch across to last 9 sts, [dc2tog over next 2 dc, dc2tog in next ch-2 sp] twice, dc in 3rd ch of turning ch, do not turn (28 dc).

Rows 29–32: Rep Rows 25–28 (twice) (20 sts). Fasten off, leaving an 18" (45.7cm) sewing length.

Finishing
With yarn needle and sewing length, matching Row 32 with base of Row 1, whipstitch Fronts to bottom edge of Back.

Armhole Edging
Round 1: With RS facing, join yarn with sc in end of 1st Broomstick Lace row on Left Front armhole edge, sc in same sp, skipping all sc rows, work 2 sc in each row-end st around armhole; join with sl st in 1st sc (64 sc).

Round 2: Ch 4 (counts as dc, ch 1), dc in same st, (dc, ch 1, dc) in each st around; join with sl st in 3rd ch of beg ch-4. Fasten off.

Rep Armhole Edging around other armhole.

Front Edging

Round 1: With RS facing, working across opposite side of foundation ch on bottom edge of Back, join yarn with sc in 1st ch, sc in each ch across, skipping all sc rows, work 2 sc in each row-end st across Right Front edge, sc in each st and each ch across Back neck edge, skipping all sc rows, work 2 sc in each row-end st across Left Front edge; join with sl st in 1st sc.

Round 2: Ch 1, sc in each of 1st 63 sts across bottom edge of Back, (dc, ch 1, dc) in each st across Right Front, Back neck and Left Front edges; join with sl st in 1st sc.

Lower Back Edging

Row 1: Working across Back bottom edge only, working in blps only, sc in 1st st, *sc2tog over next 2 sts**, sc in next st; rep from * across, ending last rep at ** (42 sts). Fasten off.

Finishing

Weave in ends.

STITCH DIAGRAM

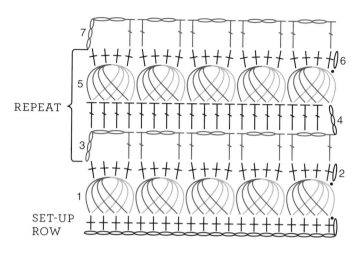

REPEAT

SET-UP ROW

REDUCE SAMPLE OF PATTERN

SHRUG LAID FLAT (BEFORE SEAMING)

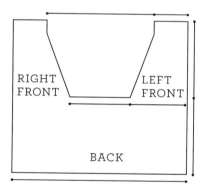

RIGHT FRONT

LEFT FRONT

BACK

SHRUG WHEN SEAMED

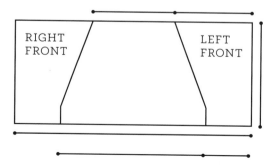

RIGHT FRONT

LEFT FRONT

HOW TO MAKE BROOMSTICK LACE

1. Crossing your hook and needle like swords, insert the needle in the loop where the hook had been.

2. With the loop not too loose and not too tight on the needle, insert the crochet hook in the next stitch, yarn over and pull up a loop.

3. Make the loop big, place it on the needle and leave it there.

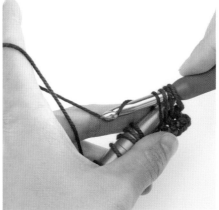

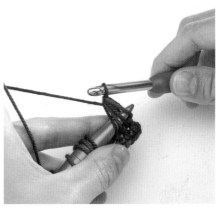

4. Repeat across the fabric, placing one big loop on the needle for each stitch.

5. When all the loops are on the needle, insert the hook under the last four loops that were placed and yarn over.

6. Pull the yarn through all four big loops at the same time, slip stitching them together.

7. Yarn over and pull through two loops on the hook, making a single crochet.

8. Place three more single crochet in the same four big loops next to the first single crochet.

FINISHED SIZE:

› 4¾" × 3½" (12.1cm × 8.9cm), not including strap

MATERIALS

› Classic Elite Yarns, Color By Kristin (1.8 oz/ 93 yds/85m/50g per ball): 1 skein each of #3248 Deep Blue Sea (A), #3215 Spring Green (B), #3232 Raspberry (C), #3236 Mushroom (D)

› Size I/9 (5.5mm) crochet hook or size needed to obtain gauge

› Locking stitch markers

› Yarn needle

› 4" (10.2cm) zipper or 7" (17.8cm) zipper cut down to size

› Sewing needle

› Matching thread

› Superglue (optional)

› Chain (optional)

GAUGE

› 18 sts = 4¾" (12.1cm); 13 rows sc = 3½" (8.9cm)

› Take time to check gauge

Souvenir Coin Pouch

You'll treasure this little bag as much as the treasures you put in it. Our daughter would likely fill her Souvenir Coin Pouch with her collection of flattened embossed pennies from the numerous zoos and museums we've visited. Practice your tapestry crochet skills with this study in pattern and color. Learn to insert a zipper too!

PATTERN NOTES

To change color in single crochet, insert the hook in the next stitch and yarn over; pull up a loop, drop the first color, pick up the second color and draw through the two loops on the hook.

Only two colors are used per round. When not using a color, work over it until it is needed again.

Rounds are worked in a spiral without joining. Place a marker in the first stitch of each round and move it as the work the progresses.

POUCH

With A, ch 19.

Round 1: Sc in 2nd ch from hook and in each ch across, rotate to work across opposite side of foundation ch, sc in each ch across, do not join (36 sc). Round 1 of chart complete.

Round 2: *With A, sc in next 3 sts, with B, sc in next 3 sts; rep from * around. Round 2 of chart complete.

Rounds 3–12: Work in sc following Chart for color changes, working from A to B (6 times).

Round 13: With D, sc2tog over next 2 sts, (pm in the new sc2tog to mark where the wrist strap will go), sc in each of next 16 sts, sc2tog over next 2 sts, sc in each of rem 16 sts; join with sl st in 1st sc (34 sts). Fasten off.

WRIST STRAP

With C, ch 36.

Make sure the length fits over your wrist. Add chains to make it longer. If you are going to felt your pouch, make the handle a little longer by adding about 12 sts because it will also shrink during the felting process.

Row 1: Sc in 2nd ch from hook and in each ch across, turn.

Row 2: Ch 1, sc in each sc across. Fasten off, leaving an 8" (20.3cm) sewing length.

Fold handle matching 1st st to last st and using tail and yarn needle, sew ends of Strap to marked st on top of bag. Weave in ends.

Note: If you like, you can felt the bag before you cut and sew the zipper.

ZIPPER

Cut the zipper to fit ¼" (6.3mm) longer than the opening. Sew across end of zipper to secure it and stop the pull or secure with a dot of superglue and allow to dry.

Turn bag inside out, open zipper, pin in place. With thread and sewing needle, sew zipper to bag. Turn bag RS out. Close zipper.

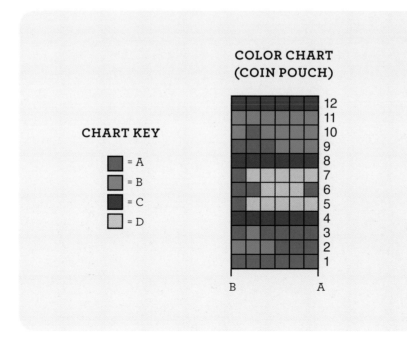

CHART KEY

= A
= B
= C
= D

COLOR CHART (COIN POUCH)

12
11
10
9
8
7
6
5
4
3
2
1

B   A

HOW TO TAPESTRY CROCHET

1. When changing color in single crochet, insert the hook into the next stitch and pull up a loop.

2. Hold the new color against the back of the fabric.

3. Yarn over with the new color.

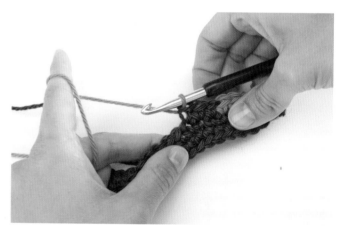

4. Pull the next color through the two loops on the hook of the old color.

5. The next single crochet made will be in the new color.

HOW TO ADD A ZIPPER

1. Turn the pouch inside out; with the zipper open, hold the zipper along the open edge of the pouch.

2. With a sewing needle and thread, sew the zipper into place. Sew both sides of the zipper, then turn it right-side out.

Impressions Hairpin Ascot

Let this gorgeous ascot be your first impression of hairpin lace crochet. You'll fall in love with this fast and meditative technique. This beginner pattern is so much fun, it may become your go-to gift for the next holiday season.

FINISHED SIZE
› 3¼" × 24½" (8.3cm × 62.2cm), unstretched
› 31" (78.7cm) long when stretched flat

MATERIALS
› Red Heart Soft Yarn (4 oz/204 yds/ 187m/113g per skein): 1 skein #9941 Watercolors
› Hairpin lace loom
› Size I/9 (5.5mm) crochet hook or size needed to obtain gauge
› Yarn needle

GAUGE
› 11 loops = 4" (10.2cm)
› Take time to check gauge

PATTERN NOTES

Strip is made first then an edging is added.

Special Stitches

Picot: Ch 3, hdc in 3rd ch from hook.

ASCOT

Set loom to 3" (7.6cm) following directions on loom package. Make 66 lps per side. Inc length by working a multiple of 3 lps (see photos 1–8).

Put in life lines on each side, remove strip from loom. (see photos 9–16).

Edging Row 1: With RS facing, starting at the bottom and working on the right side, insert hook in 1st 3 lps, work a sc, *picot, ch 3, insert hook in next 3 lps, work a sc; rep from * across to final group, ending with (sc, picot, sc) in last 3 lps. (22 sc; 21 picots; 21 ch-3 sps) Fasten off (see photos 17–22).

Edging Row 2: For the left side, with RS facing, starting at top left corner, rep Edging Row 1 (22 sc; 21 picots; 21 ch-3 sps). Fasten off.

Finishing

Weave in ends.

EDGING STITCH DIAGRAM (REDUCED SAMPLE)

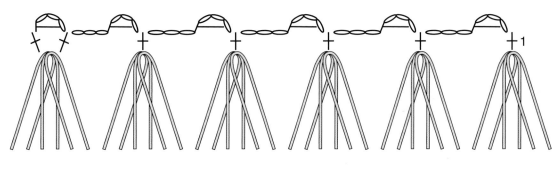

HOW TO MAKE HAIRPIN LACE

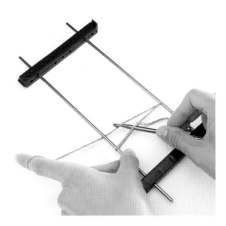

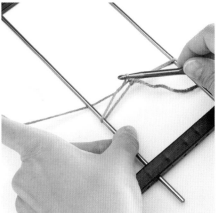

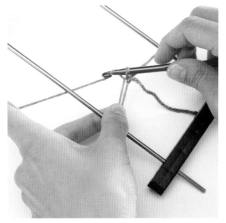

1. Place a slip knot on the left prong of the loom. Let the slip knot be loose so that the knot is in the middle between the prongs. Wrap the working yarn across the front of the loom to the right and around the back.

2. Insert the hook in the slip knot to the left of the knot.

3. Yarn over the working yarn and pull it through the slip knot.

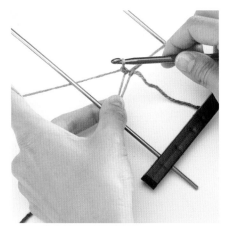

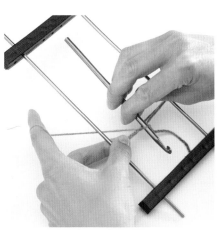

4. Chain one (for the first stitch only).

5. Turn the hook counterclockwise so that the handle points up.

6. Flip the handle of the hook downward in between the loom prongs.

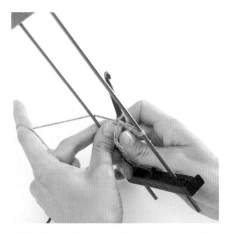

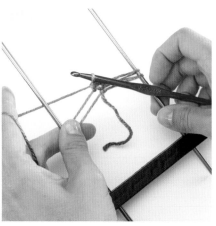

7. Hold the hook and loom in the right hand and turn both as one, as if you were turning to the next page in a book, still holding the working yarn in the other hand.

8. For subsequent stitches, insert the hook to the left of the last stitch, under the front strand of the big loop around the left prong, yarn over and pull up a loop, yarn over and pull through two loops, creating a single crochet.

9. When there are many loops on the loom and there is no room for more, take waste yarn and a yarn needle and thread a lifeline along the right prong.

10. When the waste yarn is through all the loops on the right prong, cut the waste yarn and tie the cut end to the beginning end.

11. Repeat the lifeline for the second side. (It makes sense to count the loops at this point and put the same number of loops on each lifeline.)

12. Open the bottom of the loom.

13. Slide the work down off the loom until just a few loops remain.

14. Close the bottom of the loom.

15. Resume working, adding more loops as needed.

16. The stitches will not be stacked directly above one another.

17. Insert hook under three loops at one time.

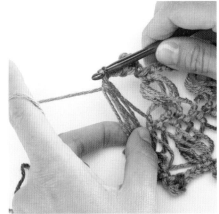

18. Yarn over and pull the yarn through the three loops.

19. Yarn over and pull through two loops on the hook, creating a single crochet.

20. To make a picot, chain three.

21. Finish the picot by placing a half double crochet in the third chain from the hook.

22. Continue in the next three loops and across the side.

DESIGNER TIP

If you have one more loop on one prong than the other, turn and add one more to the other side to even it up.

ABOUT THE AUTHOR

Ellen has been crocheting since she was ten. Her first design was a three-dimensional Rubik's Cube made of granny squares. From there, her fondest crochet memory is crocheting a blanket with her mother for her grandmother's birthday. Ellen can't remember exactly who taught her to crochet but believes that it seeped into her consciousness from an early age from her Great Aunt, Tante Margaret, who resided next door.

Before becoming the editor of *Crochet!* magazine, Ellen sold more than 250 designs and published numerous times in many crochet magazines and books. Ellen is a cast member on the PBS TV show: *Knit and Crochet Now!* and teaches for Annie's Online Classes. She has an active blog at GoCrochet.com and a busy Ravelry group. Ellen is the author of *Go Crochet! Afghan Design Workbook* (Krause Publications, 2011) and Learn Bruges Lace (AnniesCatalog.com, 2012), and is coauthor of *Crocheting Clothes Kids Love* (Creative Quayside Publishing, 2014). Follow her as GoCrochet on Facebook, Ravelry and Twitter.

When not crocheting, Ellen enjoys reading, knitting, running and chocolate cake. Ellen lives near Cincinnati with her husband, Tom, and their two children.

Index

www.fwmedia.com

18 17 16 15 14   5 4 3 2 1

Distributed in Canada by Fraser Direct
100 Armstrong Avenue
Georgetown, ON, Canada L7G 5S4
Tel: (905) 877-4411

Distributed in the U.K. and Europe by F+W MEDIA INTERNATIONAL
Brunel House, Newton Abbot, Devon, TQ12 4PU, England
Tel: (+44) 1626 323200, Fax: (+44) 1626 323319
E-mail: postmaster@davidandcharles.co.uk

Distributed in Australia by Capricorn Link
P.O. Box 704, S. Windsor NSW, 2756 Australia
Tel: (02) 4560-1600   Fax: (02) 4577-5288
E-mail: books@capricornlink.com

Edited by Noel Rivera
Design and photography by Rachael Ward, Rae by Day
Production coordinated by Greg Nock

CROCHET HOOK CONVERSIONS

US SIZE	DIAMETER (MM)
B/1	2.25
C/2	2.75
D/3	3.25
E/4	3.5
F/5	3.75
G/6	4
H/8	5
I/9	5.5
J/10	6
K/10½	6.5
L/11	8
M/13, N/13	9
N/15, P/15	10
P/Q	15
Q	16
S	19

US CROCHET		UK CROCHET
slip stitch (sl st)	• or	slip stitch (sl st)
single crochet (sc)	+	double crochet (dc)
half-double crochet (hdc)	T	half-double
double crochet (dc)	⊤	treble (tr)
treble crochet (tr)	⊤	double crochet (dc)

Notes:

* Gauge (what UK crocheters call tension) is measured over 4" (10.2cm) in single crochet (except for Lace [0], which is worked in double crochet).

** US hook sizes are given first, with UK equivalents in parentheses.

*** Steel crochet hooks are sized differently from regular hooks—the higher the number, the smaller the hook, which is the reverse of regular hook sizing.

METRIC CONVERSION CHART

TO CONVERT	TO	MULTIPLY BY
Inches	Centimeters	2.54
Centimeters	Inches	0.4
Feet	Centimeters	30.5
Centimeters	Feet	0.03
Yards	Meters	0.9
Meters	Yards	1.1

GET STITCHING WITH THESE OTHER GREAT CROCHET TITLES!

Go Crochet! Afghan Design Workbook
Ellen Gormley

Go Crochet! Afghan Design Workbook gives you everything you'll need to make beautiful afghans any time (and any place) you desire. Learn the tools and materials you'll need, along with basic crochet techniques. Next, try any of fifty mix-and-match crochet motifs in a wide variety of shapes with skill levels ranging from beginner to advanced. All crochet patterns are available in both chart and text form. Fifty afghan patterns show you how to achieve a variety of effects with a single motif, two to three motifs and finally multiple motifs, for a fun patchwork appearance.

ISBN-13: 978-1-4402-0907-9
SRN: Z6649

Beastly Crochet
23 Critters to Wear and Love
Brenda K. B. Anderson

In *Beastly Crochet*, you'll find twenty-three accessories, toys and garments featuring furry monsters, carnivorous plants, killer robots and menacing tiki figures. Learn how to tackle sewing and appliqué techniques, including how to install zippers, as well as subtle tricks for achieving personality in your critters.

ISBN-13: 978-1-5966-8574-1
SRN: 13CR01

CHECK OUT CROCHETME.COM FOR MORE CROCHET FUN!